FOUR WHEELS FIVE CORNERS

Also by Paul Wood:

FALSE CONFESSIONS: A LIFE IN HAWAI'I

SPELL OF THE SEA WITCH

LURIGANCHO
  with Edward Padilla

FOUR WHEELS
FIVE CORNERS

Facts of Life in Upcountry Maui

Second Edition

PAUL WOOD

Robyn —
I hope This will
illuminate your
next visit to The
Mountain.
Paul Wood

FLYING RABBIT PRESS
Maui, Hawai'i

Flying Rabbit Press
P.O. Box 880949
Pukalani, HI 96788

paulwoodwriter.com

ISBN 0-961443-5-5 (first edition)
ISBN 978-0-9706200-3-3 (second edition)

Second edition produced by John Dependahl, philosopher and teacher nonpareil.

Karen Bacon (www.karenannbacon.com) re-created this book's original design and prepared this edition for printing.

Artist Valentin Miro created the new chapter vignettes for this edition. Miro is presently a student at School of the Art Institute of Chicago. He exhibits his work in both Chicago and Hawai'i.

Original design contributions by Patt Narrowe, Chris Magee, and of course Barbara.

This second edition includes one additional story, all new vignettes, and numerous information updates that are presented as footnotes. Maui changed steadily and dramatically during the interval between editions. This island may run short on toilet paper, drinking water, farm produce, or prime coastal real estate, but it has one resource that just grows and grows— the good old days.

All of these pieces first appeared in the now-defunct *Haleakala Times* newspaper. I'm telling you, *those* were the days....

Printed in the United States of America

"It was reckoned a virtue for a man to take a wife, to bring up his children properly, to deal squarely with his neighbors and his landlord, to engage in some industry such as farming, fishing, house-building, canoe-making, or to raise swine, dogs and fowls."

David Malo
Hawaiian Antiquities

CONTENTS

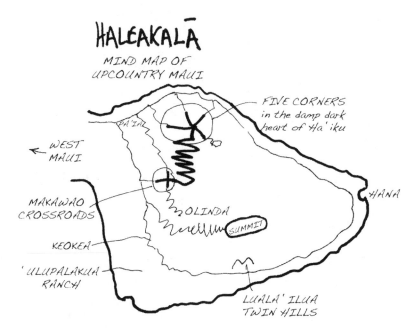

HALEAKALĀ

MIND MAP OF
UPCOUNTRY MAUI

FIVE CORNERS
in the damp dark
heart of Ha'iku

PĀ'IA

WEST
MAUI

HANA

MAKAWAO
CROSSROADS

OLINDA

SUMMIT

KEOKEA

'ULUPALAKUA
RANCH

LUALA'ILUA
TWIN HILLS

INTRODUCTION

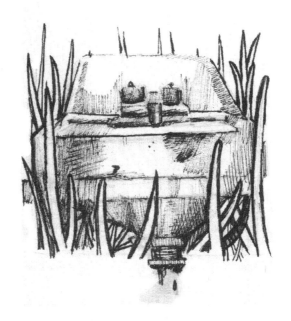

Dead Bomb Shelter
and other timely notices

Dead Bomb Shelter
and other timely notices

Everyone in Hawai'i can tell you about the good old days. For instance, everyone knows that this island, Maui, used to be a lot better. Some say it was two hundred years ago.

Some say it was two.

There are as many versions of the good old days as there are people to pretend to remember them. And I'd like you to know about mine:

The Makawao dump closed nearly four years ago, and my life has felt a little clogged up ever since.

The Makawao dump! You had to drive down into a gulch to get there, bouncing between pineapple fields with their million dagger-like leaves bristling into the Earth-blue air.

The road was so bad you didn't ever want to risk it with a passenger car even though people did that all the time. You always saw at least one old van down there packed with beer cans and banana trash, the owner parked longways to the mildly frightening community trash heap and pitchforking his waste out the sliding door. You watched rickety trailers back into a slot, weaving on the pivot of rusted-out Datsun hatchback bumpers.

You ran into plenty of trucks, too. Lots of them.

That's where we, the rooted people of Upcountry Maui, used to meet as equals, backing up with all the household poop, careful not to get too close together nor to take up too much space along the ever-shifting shoreline of waste. Neighbor toed the line with neighbor for the same humbling task in the hot gritty breeze, in the squealing din of the Cat's metal treads as it joggled the startled earth, as the white egrets leaped into the clean sky.

Dumps, like public bathrooms, are truly democratic. No one can cop an attitude at the dump. Nobody's poop is any better than anyone else's poop.

In the old Makawao dump we'd pass brooms around. Sometimes some reasonably good scrap lumber or an armload of red ti stalks would go right from one guy's truck into his neighbor's. The good old days.

These days I recycle.

I wait till no one's around and no one's listening to me mutter and gripe. Alone, I learn the sagging weight of each month's sack of beer bottles. I stagger under it, unseen and insignificant in my own back yard.

I preserve my family's poop—sort it, critique it, revisit it, package it, carry it out to the edge of my lawn at dawn on the appointed day. Strangers come, usually when I'm not looking, and then slink away taking my sorted poop to someplace I never ever go.

I wash my dog food cans and save them for weeks. I'm saving the planet. Fine. I just don't want to be seen doing this in public. I'm not going to get together with a bunch of other guys and stand there, elbow to elbow, recycling. (What—Mel, you think this aluminum or what?" "Can't tell. Got a magnet?") The whole idea is just too sad.

The Makawao dump was never sad.

I remember meeting one of my Portuguese neighbors there who complained that the dump was filling up and it was all because of the haoles, the white people from the Mainland, all those haoles who don't know what to do with their 'opala, their trash. In his mind all of Maui's troubles, including this problem with the dump, began with one major historical tragedy.

Statehood.

He was nostalgic for the life before 1959. Others I know are nostalgic for life under the monarchy, before the businessmen/traitors stole the kingdom and gave it to America. Others think life got all screwy back in 1778 when Captain Cook showed up.

We all do it.

We all yearn for some kind of past goodness—or we're nostalgic for a future goodness, or we wish the present was like the way we WISH the present was.

Tut tut tut.

I may be partial to dumps, but I have my limits. You can't start talking about Heaven now, not while you and I are both cleaning the outhouse. No. I write these essays for reasons more elevated than any make-believe nostalgia. I write them in the spirit of the Dead Bomb Shelter sign.

That sign stands over a paving dip in downtown Makawao, and it warns you not to trip on the dip. It should say "KEEP LEFT." That would be the usual thing—"KEEP LEFT" surrounded by fluorescent–colored tape draped on stanchions made from one-inch PVC pipe bolted onto plywood squares, like a bad sculpture installation produced by the post-perestroika artistic counterculture of Lithuania.

In fact, I have noticed that nearly all signs work like a "KEEP LEFT" sign. ONE WAY. YIELD. STOP. MAKAWAO 2 MILES. They all move us around in space.

But the Dead Bomb Shelter sign doesn't move us around in space. It moves us in time.

It tells a brief story. CAUTION: DEAD BOMB SHELTER, it says. It describes a bomb shelter that once lay right under the concrete paving, right under your feet. The bomb-shelter hole got backfilled. Then the freshly moved dirt did that dirty trick of settling. That's why the dip.

The sign transforms that obscure but particular spot from a glitch in the masonry to an archeological site. It reminds us to see and to live even as we rush around town. It helps to compensate for the grievous loss of the community-building Makawao dump.

It's a timely notice.

I wrote these essays to be timely notices, too.

These essays are not designed to travel efficiently through space. When they make a turn, it's generally a hairpin turn—just like the road that twists past my driveway here in the gulch country of this wave-bashed mountain. Along the road you'll find the most harmonious mix of incomplete unlike-liness. Here in this loose community of seventeen cultures where cattle graze under coconut trees, breakfast might well turn out to be Spam musubi and a donut, chased by a small tub of wheat-grass juice.

My neighbors manage to make good sense out of strange ingredients that life keeps handing them, and I'd be happy to have said that I did the same.

For the sake of this collection, let's just say that I learned my trade at the Makawao dump where everything was honest and solid—though it was transforming before your very eyes from chattel to compost! And everything was welcome, no matter how it arrived.

And in that mess a glorious work was accomplished. A community. And the community grew—not because of the artful piles of rubbish but because of the universal kindness that sits like a secret pearl inside the crusty oyster of the human heart.

I'd be satisfied if these essays served as much use.*

★ After I wrote those words above, the "Dead Bomb Shelter" sign disappeared. Now they've got an efficient little drain in the former puddle, and no one will have to be inconvenienced by noticing. I'm telling you. First the haoles took away our bomb shelter, then they took away the sign. But for those of us who remember the "Dead Bomb Shelter" sign—now THOSE were the good old days!

THE PLACE

Makawao from
twenty thousand feet
in the air

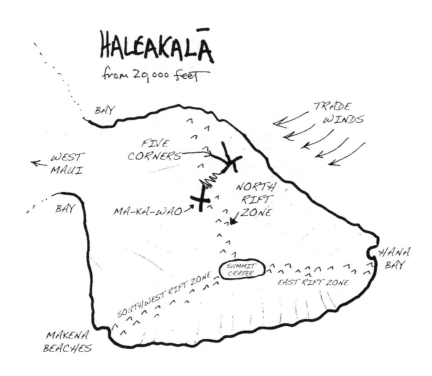

Makawao from
twenty thousand feet in the air

"It's all in how you see it!" says geologist Earl Onaga as we rise straight into the sky above the Makawao crossroads. "Most of the time people only get the close-up view of things—buildings, streets, other people, themselves. That's the problem. They don't know where they are because they can't see it. That's why they get scared!"

"Holy cow, Earl, I'm pretty scared right now."

I'm gripping the side of this two-person bucket that's shooting into space, and he seems to think this is funny. He's grinning, anyway. With certain people you can't tell if they're laughing inside or preparing to commit harakiri. That's this guy with his big white teeth, bulbous mirrorized sunglasses, and puffy high-altitude jacket with letters printed on the back: "Science blows your mind—and then you die!"

You have to watch what you ask for.

I set out to write about Makawao, which is arguably the central town—though it's not really a town—of the convoluted East Maui mountainside where I live. I thought it was a good plan to describe the town from a wide variety of viewpoints. How a merchant sees the town, how a painter sees it, how a cop....

When I asked Earl to give me the physical geography perspective, he talked me into this "Gravity Resistant Sky-Popper," a little bucket that's shooting us straight up by means of a technology that has only been tested twice in Antarctica and once by members of the rock band Fleetwood Mac.* I should have specified a walking tour.

           * Now THOSE were the good old days!

"How high are we going?"

"About twenty thousand feet is all," says Earl calmly. "About twice the height of the summit of Haleakala."

"Swell."

My ears are popping like champagne corks at an inaugural ball. The towns and roads below are disappearing, and the patterns of trees and fields start to coalesce. Now Makawao is little more than a dark green cross formed by treetops. I see rumpled, golden-green pastures. Designer-drawn, almost violet pineapple fields. Thick dark fur patches of forest.

Earl's happy. "Not a cloud! What a day!" he says. "Now, look for the big patterns."

"Looks pretty random to me."

"That's 'cause we're not high enough. Gotta go WAY up."

"Swell."

By the time we finally stop, the sky is purple. East Maui looks about the size of a turkey platter. My knees are waggling against each other and my face feels like plate of ice pressed against the front of my skull.

"Excellent," says Earl. "Now you'll see. Ignore West Maui, that's a separate mountain. Focus on Haleakala. Now tell me. What shape is it?"

"Kinda round."

"No."

I look again.

"It's three-sided."

"Excellent!"

"Can we go now?"

"In fact, Haleakala is a three-sided pyramid. It has three fairly flat faces separated by three long ridges that radiate out from the summit to the sea. See them? Those three ridges are called rift zones—long, kind of torn-up edges where lava boiled out whenever the volcano was active."

"I see lots of bumps along each of the rift zones, like pimples."

"Now you're getting the picture. Those are cinder cones,

sure signs of volcanic activity. 'Puʻu' is the proper word for cinder cones. Poo-oo. The puʻu run along the rift zones, and the rifts give the mountain its three-faced personality."

"What exactly do you mean by a 'personality?'"

"What's a personality? Let's see. I'd say it's an extreme, apparently gratuitous, and perfectly symbolic expression of unique identity. How would *you* define the term 'personality?'"

"You know, Earl, I left my coffee mug down on the ground down there. What would it take to go get it?"

"Good answer. Now check out the southwest rift zone. It goes right through Polipoli Forest, right through ʻUlupalakua Ranch, and right down to Makena Beach."

"Oh boy."

"That's why we have a Big and Little Beach at Makena. The rift zone runs down there."

"Naked people."

"You can't see them from up here."

"I know, Earl. It's just that my teeth are chattering."

"Now check out the east rift zone. It runs straight down to Hana."

"Where's Hana now."

"See that perfectly circular bay? So pretty."

"Yeah. Looks like a teeny emerald bead. But it's not exactly on the rift line. It's to the left."

"Correct. The east rift zone runs right down to a cinder cone called Ka Iwi O Pele, Pele's bones, right next to Koki Beach. Now run your eyes to the left all along the 'Hana Road' side of the volcano. See how green it is? The trade winds always hit this face of the pyramid, so it's always rainy and blasted by weather. Now look over here to the left where you live, toward the third edge of the pyramid."

"Everything is green on the Hana side, but once you cross the ridge it's not so green."

"Correct. The trade-wind storms slide along the windward

face of the mountain, but when they reach the north rift-zone ridge, they break up and settle down."

"You're saying that I live where the weather collides, crashes, and settles down?"

"Correct. You live along the north rift zone. Look at all those beautiful pu'u or eruption sites that jut up against the onslaught of weather, see Giggle Hill where the American GIs in World War II took advantage of Maui's naïve maidens.* And here are other pu'u on which the rich are building their dream homes."

"Home on a cinder cone. Odd choice."

"Your choice, man. Edge of the rain forest. That's what the name means. Ma-ka-wao. Brink of the wilderness. That's your town. A place that might bewilder."

"Wow," I say.

"Wao is right," he says. "Wao is the untameable wild. You're on the knife-edge. On the left side it's cactus and curbs and clear skies. On the other, people are raising tilapia in their drive-ways** and swinging from trees."

"This is so instructive, Earl. But now I yearn to be released."

"From what?"

"From the where. This is all the where I can take."

"What else *is* there but the where?"

"Spoken like a true geologist. How

---

* It is true that circa 1944 almost twenty thousand men camped at the base of the pu'u now called "Giggle Hill," young men who were readying themselves physically and mentally to fight and die in combat. These soldiers were preparing to travel by ship to utterly obscure islands in the Pacific Ocean (Iwo Jima?) and gun down young men from a small Asian country, Japan, or else be gunned down by them. How absurd this dance of slaughter must have felt to young fellows lying on cots in the teeming and rainbow-spangled forest of Ha'iku, Maui. Bob Hope entertained the troops here in a USO show. Now Bob's dead and so are most of the 4th Marine Division and certainly most of the girls who giggled with them on Giggle Hill. These days it is difficult to grow a tree in the district where they camped—concrete slabs still cover the soil where our heroes slept.

Note: There are no more naïve maidens on Maui.

Those too were the good old days.

about the when? Now I want to see the when. When I am."

"To do that you'll need something more advanced than a Gravity-Resistant Sky-Popper. What have you got?"

I take a sharp pencil out of my pocket and waggle it in the air.

He smiles. "Okay. Down we go."

"How fast does this bucket drop?" I ask.

"Hang on to your pencil."

✷✷ When my kids were tots, they used to practice real fishing by throwing lines into county ditches and concrete-lined sumps, and they would catch tilapia and throw them away. Point is, tilapia have the natural ability to thrive in a shit puddle. To say you're growing tilapia in your driveway is a Haʻiku joke. To think that tilapia has begun to replace salmon as a predominant supermarket fish purchase ought to make you stop and ponder the evolution of our own species.

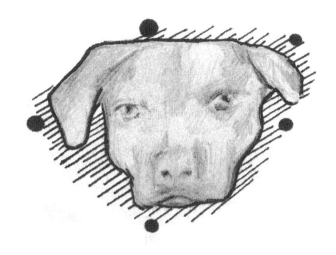

Witness reports leaping dog,
other flying beasts

Witness reports leaping dog,
other flying beasts

I quit smoking cigarettes. It's been over a week and I feel great. I could bite a piece of re-bar in half. I could arm-wrestle a backhoe. My brain's getting so much oxygen that it can't even think straight. I haven't written a paragraph in a week. Just short sentences. Very. Disconnected.

You know how it is when you blow up a balloon and pinch the end and then hold it over your head and let it go? My brain. My brain on oxygen.

So this is what it feels like—to be like all you non-smokers.

Honestly, how can you stand it? Too much oxygen is a dangerous thing. It turns breathing into a martial art, an aikido thing. One good lung-full and you're ready, just in case you need to leap into the air and kick the back of someone's head. World peace is obviously out of the question, here in this aerobic world where no peace pipes are passed. Peace may be out of the question, but I'm telling you one thing:

Nothing's gonna upset me.

I'm under control. Willpower. Nothing's gonna upset me, not even the fact that my dog's legs are too short.

In fact, the main problem I have experienced in researching this essay is the embarrassing stumpiness of my dog's legs. Plus the excess oxygen that's rattling my brain. Plus the everpresent risk that this essay will turn out to be truly pointless. Plus the chronic spinelessness of American public opinion and the near impossibility of finding true love in an increasingly fragmented, expanding universe.

Excuse me while I chew on this re-bar for a minute.

Knowing that my thought process is going to be impaired

this week, I decide to let my dog Makapuʻu write the essay instead. I decide to drive him to Makawao, then follow him around while he points out the sights and smells that most interest him. Let him do all the sustained thinking for a change.

Good plan, but for one flaw.

My dog can't jump into my truck anymore. Don't laugh. This is a serious matter when you live Upcountry.

My old truck. Now there was a jump he could make! He could fly in there like a thick-chested wolf leaping an ice-choked gorge to fetch meat to the brush-masked cave. To the future! To the rescue! Hound, leaping! Man, smoking! Ah those were the days.

My new truck is a four by four. The tailgate's higher than the old one's used to be. That's the problem. To tell the whole truth, my dog's not as svelte as he used to be. That's the other part of the problem. In fact, he's not even as svelte as my old truck used to be.

Picture a saddle thrown over a piano bench and you'll get a pretty good sense of my dog's dimensions. Evolution has not selected him as one of its soaring, leaping creatures. Even when he used to get into the old truck, he always looked so serious about it that you knew he was bluffing. You knew he was scared.

The first time I ever called him to jump into my new truck, when he tried to jump but only his front paws made it, and then when he fell, clawing away at the tailgate, that was the first time I ever realized that a dog can feel humiliated. He just walked away. That was that. He'd made a complete fool of himself, he was perfectly willing to admit it to anyone, but he wasn't going to hang around to find out who cared. He certainly wasn't going to fall on his doggie ass, his stiff little legs exposed and wiggling in the air, while attempting to jump that high ever again.

After that, I had to pick him up, all ninety-three pounds of hair and grease and Alpo, to get him into the new truck. Usually now I'll back the truck up to a grassy slope next to my driveway. What I need is a mutt-sized cattle chute.

Despite the hassle, I do like to take the dog out into the community. If you own a truck, you know why. Once we get rolling, Makapu'u goes wild with joy. He sticks his snout into the wind and sucks up, yawns up, all the smelly news of Maui and of its people and of its many cultures of dogs. His ears flap back and forth like carwash soap-slappers. His tiny round dome of a skull and the big goopy grin indicate that all his information is pretty simple and tidy.

Just what I need for this no-nicotine essay. Something that makes simple sense.

So the dog and I park on Baldwin Avenue down by Nakui Street, across from David Warren's art studio.* I drop the tailgate. The dog looks over the edge, then sits down again. He's not going to jump out. After all, how's he gonna get back in?

"Come on," I say. "Stop worrying. I've got an article to write."

The fool trusts me, and he jumps. He hits the ground running, and he goes right for the most interesting spot in the whole town of Makawao—which is a little row of croton bushes that jut from the front door of a little house on the corner of Nakui.

Underneath those bushes my dog finds ten thousand smells. He stays under there sniffing for at least fifteen minutes. I imagine that he has uncovered the entire history of Makawao, recorded in a kind of museum of smell-messages that were left by and for dogs. I've never really noticed those bushes before, but they are (for dogs, anyway) the be-all and the end-all.

When Makapu'u comes out from

* David, a grand Celt for sure, scary for his inner bigness and absolute sensual self-awareness, was the only man on Maui who could convincingly perform the role of King Lear. He died in the late 1990s, still in his prime, while taking a healthy walk on the streets of Pukalani. A speeding car came careening and smacked into him. He died as if crucified on a plumeria tree. What a death, for such a rebellious altar boy turned Gauguin visionary of naked joy dance.

* I don't know what Kris is doing these days. She was a very nice community police officer. She talked to people and smiled and laughed and never arrested anybody. Maybe we can't afford such useless jobs anymore, now that civility has been eliminated from the budget. Or maybe she has gone somewhere more unhappy in order to hit people on the head with her billy club and so justify her pay. Ten bucks for a bang on the head. A lot of people make a living like that.

** Gary Moore, that golden-hearted grouch who owned the stove shop, he's gone now, too. So is his brindle boxer Chase, who always wore a flower lei for a collar and liked to flirt with blondes. In a way the unofficial volunteer mayor of Makawao, Gary liked to monitor people's behavior up and down the street by means of an electric bullhorn. And he always organized the stick-horse race every year just before the Fourth of July parade. He's gone but the old building is still there, a boutique now. He told me that the building started as a pool hall in the

under those bushes, he's ready to go home. He's smelled it all.

"Oh no," I insist. "We're going to tour this town. Now get walking!"

Kris Dixon, the Makawao Community Police Officer, comes by.* Her office is inside that little house where the bushes are full of information. We chat. She asks how old the dog is.

"Five or six," I say. I realize that I don't know my dog's age because I never celebrate my dog's birthday. I realize for the first time how much I hate the whole tradition of counting birthdays. I'm sorry I know how old I am, and I don't want any of you counting up how many years I've wasted when my birthday comes around next time. Remember that. I'm a reformed smoker. I'm alive, that's all. I don't need to keep score.

"Five or six? Is that all?" says Officer Dixon. "Looks like he needs to jog a little bit."

Because Officer Dixon is a slender and well-meaning woman, the dog and I decide not to strike up a debate on the issue. Instead, he takes me on a short tour of Makawao. Very short. From the dog's point of view, the whole town can be summarized in the following sentences:

• The grass in front of Silversword Stoves** is full of interesting messages. Sniff there.

- A plastic bin that once held dried octopus legs is lying on the sidewalk, crushed. This is definitely the most exciting object in the entire town.

- You'll want to cross the street so that you can walk your nose right past Rodeo Store's deli counter. Then you'll want to cross back so that you can walk your nose past Komodas.

early fifties, then housed a holy-roller church. It was a gun shop and saddlery when Gary took it over, and he then converted it to a stove shop that also sold hot sauces, Hula Hottie's Cherry Chipotle Hot Chocolate Bars, and copies of my books. Now, those were the good days. All of them.

- You can lie in the shade at the crossroads, under the old gas station awning, and protect the town from traffic accidents.

That's the tour. Not very thrilling for a grouchy ex-smoker, but thrilling enough for a dog. When I call, "Let's go!" he runs back down the street, trying to leap into every car and truck in town.

When I drop the tailgate of my truck and turn around to hoist him up (somehow), he is already in the air! He's sailing past my ear in a golden blur!

He's leaping, just like a lawn mower that's trying to set a pole-vaulting record. His rear paws hit the top edge of the tailgate, and I grab the fur around his tail and boost him into the bed of the truck. The look on his face says this:

"See? It's attitude!"

Explosive leaps. Eruptions of oxygen. Flying through space in a burst of inadequate legs. This whole town, all of Upcountry Maui, is re-created every day by all of us as we stumble forth with our attitudes. I disagree with every one of you! And yet look at what we manage to agree on, every day, as if we know what we mean when we say "Makawao."

I look up and there are dogs flying everywhere—terriers, poi dogs, pit bulls, Chihuahuas, Great Danes, sailing over the store tops and the trees. Soon Holsteins and Aberdeen Angus cows are soaring through the sky, and above them appaloosas and palominos. Peace may be out of the question, but happiness on a volcanic island gets doled out in unforgettable bursts.

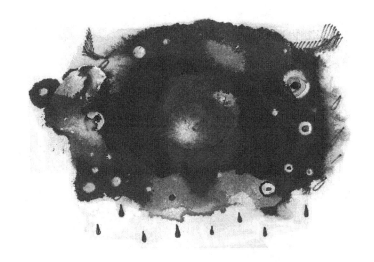

Doing our jobs
in the big rain

Doing our jobs in the big rain

A thousand kinds of rain come down on the Ha'iku side. They generally sweep in from Hana, billow up to Olinda, splash over Makawao, then break apart into the dry air as they blow toward Pukalani.

Of these, there is one kind of rain that everyone knows—that big, big....

If it kept up for two days it would wash all of us and all of our artifacts right off the face of the mountain. That's the kind I'm talking about.

I love that kind of rain.

I'm not stupid enough to think it's safe or fun. That rain once killed a friend of mine. I've seen it destroy cars. For three days I fought against it to save my own house, and I only partially succeeded.

After that my sons and some friends and I built a rock wall, a tough, gracefully curved stone shoulder thrown against any flash floods. It runs one hundred feet and stands higher than our heads where it brunts against any flood, sweeping left with a bullfighter move to fool the water past the house into a deeper gulch.

Only a handful of us can remember the re-bar and beer cans and sweat that we dropped into the wall and buried forever into mortar and rubble. Over the past four years, the wall has taken on a tawny greenish cast. Ha'iku has accepted it.

Now I look at this wall with Egyptian satisfaction. This rock monument will outlast me, and it will outlast my wooden house. I think that it might last thousands of years. Other humans will live near this wall and wonder about its builders.

Even if humans disappear it will still do what it does.

Its bow perfectly counters the water's bow, and when rock and water slide together in these big rains that I'm talking about, one holding the line and the other testing it, I don't see competition so much as a perfect agreement.

The wall grew out of an agreement that the big rain demanded.

When it's raining seriously at dawn, you know you're in for a day of such agreements. The cold rain slaps against everything, pushing against the branches so that they twist and turn. The dog keeps pacing and shifting on the deck, then drops loudly, his snout pushed into the weather, his eyes cocking back and forth. Dawn comes slow and approximate in one of those rattling gray skies.

By ten o'clock, all heaven has broken loose. Wet drumming shakes the roof. It says: if the water can't do it, then the crackling and pounding itself intends to drown us out, drown out all of our protected activities. Liquid crystal comes sheeting off the roof as if we'd built the place under a waterfall.

And then, unbelievably, the percussion-chaos gets even louder. People stop what they're doing, just stop. And then it gets louder.

The roads can never hold it all. If you live on this side, you know where the bad places will be, the temporary riverbeds and short-term ponds where you need to drive.

Each storm will dump with a different intensity on different roads. In one storm Upper Ulumalu will heave a gorge-full of dirt down into a swamped Five Corners intersection. In another a whole lake will cut you off from Hanzawa Store. Another time Pe'ahi will flood, or Kokomo Road will turn into a miles-long waterslide perfect for hydroplaning into a catastrophe.

These roads are not roads, not any longer, not when the big rain hits. They reveal themselves to be sluices, sluices we have built to hasten the destruction of this single mountain we live on, Haleakala. The pine roads, soaked to a state of truck-swallowing mush, disgorge yards and yards of fresh red earth.

The new homes too give up some of their costly acreage every time it hits like this. I always see tons of Upcountry land heading to sea when our roads turn into these sluices.

In the big picture, that's what we're doing here. We think we are building, but we're doing the opposite—eroding, upsetting, gouging loose the earth, doing the same damage as pigs only more. No matter what we build, we're doing the water's work.

Whenever I see that rich red current coursing along the roads, clogging the culverts, carrying tree parts and hubcaps, empty vodka bottles, shoes, dead chickens, but mostly earth, earth, earth, I can see it: UPCOUNTRY IS GOING DOWN.

Don't worry, though. This is not just erosion. This is inevitable. Our pig-work just hastens the inevitable. Now that the volcano has quit (supposedly),* it's only a matter of time till Haleakala gets beaten back into the sea. The mountain is inchly fleeing northward, all the while chased and beaten and then savagely beaten by kai and wai (by salt water and fresh water), sinking under its own weight and crumbling apart until that far day when it will finally dwindle into a sand shoal, or an atoll, or a rock outcropping for seabirds to mass on, fat seals to haul their fertile bodies onto.

We're here to help that happen.

★ Since this essay was first published, geophysicists from the Hawaiian Volcano Observatory visited numerous Global Positioning System sites on Haleakala in order to determine whether or not the mountain has swollen. If it has, then magma is pushing up from below and getting ready to influence the value of real estate on Maui. After all, Haleakala is still an active volcano. It last erupted as recently as 1600, about the time that Shakespeare was writing Hamlet. Back when I wrote this essay, everyone thought that Haleakala erupted in 1790, between the visits of Captain George Vancouver and the stop-by of the French explorer Jean Francois de Galaup, Compte de La Perouse, but now we know that this crazy idea derived from badly drawn coastline maps. I used to enjoy telling people the story of the eruption of 1790 and it was crap. I'm ashamed to think about how much crap I have promulgated in my day. This anthology of essays is my mea culpa.

Perhaps this is why my neighbors and I are always in a good mood, an excited state of friendliness, whenever the big rain comes down. Every guy with a backhoe is out on the road in a yellow slicker, big pinwheels of water spraying off his back tires. The linemen for the electric company go to work in the worst of it. The county road crews do heroic deeds in the downpours. I never resent my utility bills or my taxes during the big rain.

On those days, anyone who moves meets some kind of adventure. Getting into a store safely is an achievement, a shared achievement, and so is getting home again. We share a danger, but it's a danger we can manage (as long as we work together), a danger with its quiet purpose of pushing forward the water's battle, a danger that frees us from the lonely and anxious feeling that we're in charge, somehow, of the whole mess—we, with our little bills and businesses and tightly-held beliefs.

After all, you can hold water for a brief time and you can fool it into going left or right, but you can never control the stuff. Not only that, you can never really get upset with water. Despite its destructive force, water is entirely simple and innocent.

Water is a collective system of pure logic triggered by one and only one desire—downward. Any means to that end.

We can catch it, freeze it, drink it, walk it around inside our bodies, flush it, fight it, carry it, ride it, wipe it up, and drown in it—but in the end we're all doing water's job. We're all in agreement with its plan to conquer the bony inhospitable earth.

Despite all our beautiful liquid thoughts to the contrary, we're really no more than two-legged sacks of organized water stalking forth to get the job done. We are expendable, highly specialized advance troops built to take the heat of a resentful sun.

Then, when the big rain finally settles back at the end of a turbulent and truly Haʻiku day, you almost have to laugh.

This has been quite a visit. You step out into the yard. The clouds are breaking up, and some iron-hard stars are piercing through the black gaps.

You hear a distant gurgling in the hills and the gulches. The wind stirs around, and five fresh drops of the stuff fly off a banana leaf and hit you on the face. You and the land you live on. Once again you've made the agreement.

A solution to
Makawao's parking problem

A solution to
Makawao's parking problem

At sunset you can park your old buggy in Makawao without much trouble. Most everyone else has gone home—eating, or getting ready to eat, or just plain hiding out.

The sky turns rich with color then, mostly lavenders backed up with a strange orange. A car will go past maybe once a minute. After its engine rips the air and passes though, you get the weird sensation of actually noticing the town itself.

For once you hear electricity buzzing in the power poles, up at the top where they're clotted with black cables stretching every which way like bicycle spokes. All the trees speak up, rattling behind the funky shops in the gathering winds. The slam of a car door sounds four times louder than it does at noon.

The slanty parking slots in front of Rodeo Store, on the Ha'iku side of Baldwin Avenue and up close to the stop sign, those are filled. The parking places parallel to the sidewalk on the other side, from Makawao Steak House up to Silversword Stoves—those are all taken. Other than that you've got lots of choices.

That's the way our little town should be I guess. Not much happening.

At mid-day this is a whole different place. Now you've got TRAFFIC. Rams. Rangers. Broncos. Blazers. Tow trucks. Here comes Earl Calasa, banging through the intersection in his banged-up salty-red hauler, one of the hardest-working trucks on the mountain. An MEO bus turns the corner with a full load of aunties and tutus. White trucks roar out of the county base yard, king cabs with six big men and their shovels.

You have to shout above it all. Above the whining of loose

belts and the high metal whistling of worn brakes. Above the deep tuba roars of gunned engine guts. Above the scratch and bang of tires smearing the gravel and bouncing on the drain covers. Then it stops for a moment. Silence drops like a hundred dollar bill. A single mynah gets his chance and take it.

Chip. Chip. Chip.

But even in that silence, you hear the overall murmur of engines, like a sound track in a movie when you don't know why but you know something bad's about to happen. Suddenly, a hot-looking wahine in black shades and a black Datsun with black-tinted windows peels around the corner, her pounding reggae building up from the right then sinking away to your left.

Suddenly, two hundred cars are all in a knot. People are backing out where they can't see. Drivers are slaloming around a big parked Le Sabre that just couldn't pull in far enough no matter what. A rusty panel truck built like a Matson container, same thing—taking up half the roadway. The Waterman flatbed is delivering, all of his water jugs sparkling like plastic blue ice. He's blocking the fire hydrant. But he's got no choice.

Jaywalkers cross wherever they can. They go, cars stop, they stop, they go, cars go. It's a dance. Then a herd of downhill bike riders sails through, all in their poolball-green helmets nervously squeezing their handbrakes with the grim determination of somebody trying to gaff a shark in knee-high water. Their leader, riding no-handed, is turned around in his seat and shouting like a sailor, "KEEP IN LINE! DON'T LOOK BACK! ONE FALSE MOVE AND YOU'RE DEAD! ALOHA!"

Some people have called the town "dysfunctional" on account of times like this, but I disagree. Or maybe I just like dysfunctional towns. Because I've seen "functional" towns and I'll tell you what.

Functional sucks.

Say "functional," and I think of certain towns I've visited in Orange County, California, where any house is painted one of three legislated color combinations and you get a fine whenever you leave your garage door open longer than twenty minutes. In a town like that, the sidewalk alone is wider than Baldwin Avenue—on both sides of the street. And no one's walking on the sidewalk.

Everyone's driving. They're driving with windows rolled up on one of those eight extra-wide lanes that any "functional" town provides even when it has far less traffic than Makawao gets when St. Joseph's Church finishes High Mass.

To walk on those runway-sized sidewalks is to know a soul-killing loneliness. Off in the distance you glimpse an old Mexican woman, someone's servant, pushing a shopping cart and hiding inside a dark, toothless silence.

You start to walk from one side of the street to the other, and a dread feeling strikes you halfway across that asphalt Sahara. Suppose your heart gives out! Suppose you sprawl flat across one of those mirage-wet lanes, crying out with a death-shriek! Your final glance would take in the grillwork of an approaching car. Its turn indicator would click on. The car would move into some other extra-functional lane, leaving you and your dysfunctional behavior to the disposal of wee-paid municipal authorities.

If it's a parking place you want, there's the place to get one.

If you chopped Makawao into portable pieces, shipped them all to Orange County, and spread them out over a few square blocks, the whole town would simply disappear.

I count eighty-five parking spots on Makawao Avenue from the three-way stop crossroads (the very heart of confusion)* to the end of the commercial

★ Now it's a four-way stop, and so it is more functional. But for most of my life it was the only three-way stop intersection (as far as I know) in the world. By the way, the no-stop-sign direction of the old crossroads was the lane that headed straight uphill to Olinda. All the rich haoles lived up there. They must have felt real lucky that they didn't have to stop at all while driving home from the sugar plantation and mill below. Now THOSE were the good old days.

strip down by the Makawao Steak House. This includes the Komodas' lot, which is (wink wink) just for the Komodas. In that stretch we have about thirty businesses.

And how many cars go through town every day? I'm sure someone's got the official count, but who cares. Suppose we figure one car every five seconds for the twelve busiest traffic hours of the day. That's eight thousand six hundred and forty. Add a bit more for the other twelve hours—call it ten thousand a day.

Ten thousand! What a beautiful big figure! What a voluptuous town! What a miracle!

Suppose that one day, maybe today, every one of those ten thousand people showed up in town and tried to park at the exact same moment. Every available parking spot in Makawao would have about a hundred and twenty cars waiting for it. Picture cars piled on cars nearly six hundred feet high, higher that any high-rise tower in Honolulu. If that ever happens, I hope to heaven that I'll be there.

In fact, I will be there. After all, who are those ten thousand people?

Us. The most diverse group of ten thousand you could assemble anywhere on this planet. Pig farmers and preachers, plumbers, pizza-makers, punks, and pineapple pickers. Cowpokes and cruisers, clerks, accountants, and clothes merchants. Not to mention the alarming mix of races, language, creeds, ages, cares, histories. You know what I'm talking about.

Makawao makes us mix. Unlike many other towns, it serves this special purpose. Starting with the stop, where we have to halt, halt again, wave at each other, guess what each other will do, cuss under our breaths, thank each other, the whole trip through town is an exercise in community interaction. Every trip makes us test our prejudices and look each other in the face.

If Baldwin Avenue was a streamlined multi-lane thoroughfare, would we ever do that—look each other in the face? If we could zip through town, would we be a better community?

Go ahead and laugh if you like, but here's my truth. I like the inconvenience. I like that we all have to take care of each other while we back in and out of broken driveways, remember how to parallel park while eight waiting drivers make wisecracks, and bend the law while we jaywalk—meanwhile, don't forget, we're all taking care of that guy's extra-long LeSabre.

I'm telling you my solution to the parking problem. Take it. Take it as an exercise in community fitness.

If all of us did (and most of us do), we'd be in heaven. Because I guess that heaven is a loud, disorganized, and—above all—wonderfully dysfunctional place.

☾

My town, its parade,
its parade, and its parade

My town, its parade,
its parade, and its parade

At the appointed time and day, people in my community go to the town's busiest street and, standing or sitting, block up the sidewalks.

They wear clothing that they wouldn't normally wear in public—for example, a cowboy hat that on every other day of the year sits on the high shelf in the closet.

This year a man tied the string of a helium balloon to the adjustment strap on the back of his baseball cap. I don't believe this man would do such a thing on any normal day—stand around on the street with a balloon floating over his head.

(But you know, I can't be sure of that. In my town people will wear turbans, lava-lavas, chaps, string bikinis, live animals, aura-sensitive crystal tiaras, hip boots, glitter—even balloons, both partly and fully inflated—on any given day of the week.)

On this appointed day, as I was saying, some people clump on the sidewalk while other people walk or ride slowly along the middle of the street so that they can be looked at.

This is called a parade.

The distinction between the people who do nothing on the sidewalks and the people who pass in front of them is so important that a bright yellow plastic tape marks the symbolic border between them. Black letters in the tape spell, repeatedly, "Crime Scene Do Not Pass."

The purpose of a parade is to give lots of people the chance to look at other people without much of a chance that they'll look back. We humans love to do that. (What else are the movies all about, then, if you don't really think so?)

If you're willing to take the walk, people will spend a whole morning standing on a public street wearing a balloon just to have the chance to look at you when you do that.

At least, in my town on the Fourth of July that's what we like to do. We also like to look at horses. (In some cases, we prefer to look at horses.)

We on the sidewalks all have one reason to be there, and one alone—to stare impolitely from behind sunglasses and say anything we want without caring who hears. The rest of the year we keep our eye contact to quick glances and keep our thoughts to ourselves, but this is a holiday. On holidays, social order breaks down; that's why we have holidays.

On the holiday called Independence Day, we get to look until our appetites are crammed. Such pleasure does not make us independent, but it does make us feel free. According to a recent Gallup poll, seventy-two percent of Americans agree that, in a democracy, personal freedom is more important than equality. In my town we take the personal freedom to stare and gawk at each other on July Fourth, and some of us drink beer a little earlier in the day than usual, and that's fun.

But here's the interesting question. Why do people volunteer to march in a parade, to pass between these eyeball firing squads? Why do they want to move through the main artery of the town like some sort of vital community blood?

They have reasons. These reasons are many and complicated. This year I noticed three—as if I were watching three parades pass at once, each intermingled with the other.

The first reason would seem to be the national joy of patriotism, because the color guard comes early in the parade, borne on a black mare that prances and back-steps toward the crowd. The galvanized roofs of the town's main shops—whose wooden walls have cliffed against the tropical weather for so long that their hides have turned the texture of old leather—wear a mile-long hat band of Old Glory pennants. Everywhere we look the US flag snaps like big sparks off a car battery. Electrifying. Incapable of rest.

Because this is the theme of the parade, I keep thinking about the high ideals—independence and liberty. You'd think an island in the Pacific would be as independent as it gets. And it sure is. Until you run out of toilet paper, which we did back in the early seventies. But the barges and planes have been more reliable since. Our type of independence comes with barges.

We believe in liberty, too. Not long ago we actually liberated one of the islands in our own Maui County from a hostile government that was dropping tons of bombs on the place and shattering its fragile ecosystem. Then we forced that hostile government to clear its unexploded bombs away from one trail. Now people can walk safely from the shore to the mountaintop as long as they walk in single file. And then that hostile government simply stopped removing its myriad of other unexploded bombs from the rest of the island because it needed to go bomb other places. And that hostile government is us. I mean, the US. And that tortured island is Kahoʻolawe.

Like lots of Americans, I was born wishing for a bomb shelter. Now I have a piece of the Berlin Wall sitting on my desk. I've been through hurricanes and earthquakes and tsunamis and divorces and floods and bankruptcies and a ruptured appendix; I like harvesting bananas, or nearly anything. I am an ordinary man. I think that Dependence deserves its day, too.

As usual on July Fourth, I'm thinking too much. Forgetting the whole point. I take a lesson from my neighbor, who says to me after the color guard passes—his voice thick with Scottish snare-drum rattlings—"Not one person took off the hat when the colors walked by. Except for an alien. Me."

He looks at my cowboy hat, which is on my head, and says, "When you come here next year, please take notice of how many fucking guys forget to take off their hats when the flag goes by. It's something I've observed for twenty-eight years and I've only been a fucking citizen since eighty-one."

The national park rangers are hiking past now with brown ponies and a fine buckskin mule, the mule a rarity in these parts.

And then I begin to notice the second obvious reason people dare to parade—for the personal joy of commerce. Nearly everyone but the color guard is advertising a product or service. The staff of the physical therapy clinic lets us admire the straightness of their spines while they show us a sign that reads "We Accept All Insurance." A concrete-pumping truck rolls past. "Pumping With Confidence." The Maui Stunt Men pass by on a flatbed, pretending to beat each other silly.

Every July Fourth parade should feature this kind of shameless advertising, a great American tradition. Plus, it serves an important purpose where we live. Maui's merchants and entrepreneurs are gradually undermining the plantation economy that's kept my state in undemocratic, feudal bondage for a hundred and fifty years. And yet—now here I go, thinking again—shameless advertising has nothing to do with independence. These people want us to need their well-massaged tendons, their well-pumped grout, and their well-faked disasters. They want us to depend on them.

In a truly independent community, would anyone at all show up for a parade?

Suddenly, a limousine service drives one of its gleaming white cars through the ogling throngs. Draped over the car, hood trunk and bumper, six good-looking women wear nothing but tiny Star-and-Stripes bikinis.

My neighbor starts in again. "And there's another thing. You should never wear the fucking flag! Not even if... not that I..." But his voice trails off because he's concentrating so hard on the many images of Old Glory.

And then right behind the bikinis steps the Salvation Army, ranks of somber young women, mostly Filipina, marching in derbies and straight, past-the-knee skirts.

The Parade Marshals, who decided on the sequence of the parade entries, have a sense of humor.

I notice the Parade Marshals now, sitting with dignity on their accommodating horses. Suddenly, the rest of the parade with its bikinis and balloons looks a little frivolous. After all, these men and women on horseback actually own this parade. They and their people have siphoned down and up from their families' ranches and gulches, and they're walking the gauntlet with grace and dignity, adults among children, heading for their rodeo grounds one mile up the hill.

They've replaced the police today, and they're governing their own town from horseback. They aren't kidding. They're not selling anything, and I don't believe they're thinking much about the Republican agenda on Capitol Hill, nor about documents signed two hundred and twenty years ago by somebody else's grandfather.

If I can guess their reason, a third reason for accepting the curious stares of all, it's this:

They come to reclaim the town.

They are the conscience of the land made visible; they are the rooted people. The affairs of town can't possibly rattle them. Double the number of shops? Tear them all down? These questions can't possibly strike at the heart of their experience of community.

Roots don't grow under shop roofs. They grow in soil mulched by the bodies of all who have gone before, pressed flat by hoofs and strong feet, watered with perspiration.

Our parade ends with street-sweeping trucks wire-whisking the roadway, stirring up a perfume of horse dung, asphalt, hot leather, crushed leaves. The machines are chased by a dragonfly that bobs up into a wide sky, a sky that's as blue and confident as a freshly washed razor.

This parade, I realize, has nothing to do with independence.

The fable of the brand-new
building inspector

The fable of the brand-new building inspector

Once upon a recent time, an earnest young man came to Maui from Seattle, Washington. He just wanted to be free, live simply, have a good job, swim in the sea. He was tired of city life with all of its rules and controls.

In Seattle, he had worked as a building inspector. Maui, he could see, had many buildings that deserved inspection. Life on Maui would work more smoothly, he could tell, with more careful application of certain perfectly sensible rules and controls.

He had the clear-eyed madness of any newcomer. He carried his rulebook like a missionary. Some time previous, missionaries from New England had convinced the people of Maui to hide their behavior behind closed doors. Now this inspector would consult his rulebook to specify exactly which kinds of doors to hide behind.

So the young man landed a job inspecting buildings for the County of Maui. For his first assignment, the chap was assigned to the under-inspected crossroads town of Makapiapia.

As he drove into Makapiapia, he could see the town for what it was. He didn't even have to get out of his truck for that. He could see that Makapiapia was a living testimony to the enduring power of corrugated tin roofing.

He was not fooled by the Western-style cut-out facades on the front of each store. He started looking past the High-Noon porches pasted to the dry plywood fronts of all the shops.

He was not charmed by the fresh paint on the few shops that had slapped it on, like old ladies who had smeared on bright lipstick even though they could no longer find the edges of their lips.

He saw that if you put a marble on the floor near the cash register of the general store, the marble would roll spontaneously down the aisle between the saimin packages and the sexy magazines, turn left at the taro chips, and then, just in front of the limp produce section, drop through a gap in the floor down to the bare dirt crawl space under the building where an ownerless Weimaraner slept every night.

In every board he saw dry rot and damp rot and fungus condominiums, the powdering corruptions of Time. He saw the mineral clogging of galvanized pipes, and he heard the rattling of inadequate roofing.

He saw high-voltage electrical wiring sheathed in what looked to him like peanut husks. He peeled away wallboard to find studs at four-foot intervals, more or less. He witnessed the industry of termites; he grew familiar with their terrible dungpiles. He asked to see the Certificates of Occupancy of the shopkeepers.

Only two had them.

He saw that eighty-two thousand nine hundred and seventy-six people a day stomped through these shuddering shacks, eighty-two thousand nine hundred and seventy-six dreamers and fools and philosophers, loud-voiced sensualists, bearded mystics, pig farmers, and calloused survivors, none of whom gave the whispiest damn about the terrible dungpiles.

In fact, they loved the terrible dungpiles that pointed upwards, in their tiny way, toward a human heaven.

As the wind tossed itself about the shops, and the rains coiled in and out, and the sun poured itself promiscuously anywhere, the good citizens of Makapiapia scarcely even heard the chorus of suitable whisperings that arose from all those terrible dungpiles—just so many more syllables in Time's long and appropriate language.

So the building inspector from Seattle announced that he was shutting down the entire town of Makapiapia.

That night, the merchants of Makapiapia met in a state of controlled panic, which was the only way they could ever meet. They gathered in the office of Larry Broadhurst, the chiropractor who kept a dagger strapped to his shin at all times.

There was the owner of a Chinese herbal medicine and crystal shop, three women who each imported Balinese demon masks and fake ikat fannypacks, a gelato merchant, a naturopath, and a sand-play therapist. Two oil painters and a seaweed sculptor came because they had studios in the little town. There was also the epileptic owner of a small locksmith shop and two restaurateurs—who had schemed in the car on the way over about setting up a meat boutique in the window facing the Ginseng Elixir Fountain. Leonard Breath, the colonic irrigationist who advertised "sterile disposable tips," he was there.

Not everyone came to the meeting. The florist was having a tonsillectomy. The town barber had only cussed at the building inspector, calling him a "stink haole troublemaker." That was the end of the issue for her. The long-time merchants, Japanese families, were having dinner in back of their stores; they didn't bother.

Taoana Tantra and Moondolphin, the lesbian owners of the Dust-To-Dust Maranatha Natural Food Store, had their regular prayer group to go to. A special guest was going to unveil evidence of reincarnation in the Bible. Since the philosophy of their relationship was "physical immortals do it forever," they felt the building inspector's problem was primarily a vibrational one anyway. And the guy who owned the Booze Barn didn't come because he didn't give a damn.

The meeting lasted an hour and fifteen minutes. For an hour, everyone took turns saying the same thing: they were gonna stay open until somebody shut them down.

Someone suggested an organized appeal to the county. Leonard Breath, the colonic irrigationist, volunteered to spearhead the campaign. No one offered to join him, so the idea crapped out.

Then the meeting degenerated into a gripe session about vandalism. When Larry Broadhurst tried to demonstrate how to break a man's neck with a broom handle, most people went home.

The next day, Makapiapia opened quietly.

Shopkeepers scanned the street. They walked back and forth to each other's shops, then stood side-by-side, scanning.

"Nothing's going to happen," said one. "What could they do?" said the other.

"Nobody'd shut down a whole town!"

"Do you think?"

The gelato merchant put in a call to the governor's office, but then hung up when someone answered the phone.

In fact, nothing happened all day. Or ever. Except for this:

The building inspector from Seattle was quickly removed to a new position. He was placed in charge of a mobile unit dispatched by the county animal shelter.

He came back for the ownerless Weimaraner, but the citizens of Makapiapia drove him away. Later, he went into business for himself, offering a Home Buyers Inspection Service. Then his wife left him for a part-Hawaiian pot grower (also part owner of the Pono Pump Gym), who shot the tires off his pickup truck when he was chasing the renegade lovers through a cane field under a sickle moon.

After that, the building inspector moved back to Seattle.

❨

THE PRICE

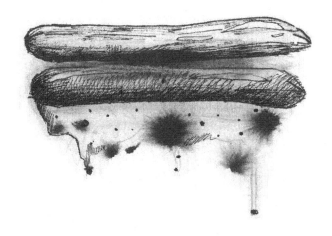

Crime Watch:
the impossible
does not come true

Crime Watch:
the impossible does not come true

If it isn't easy, it's impossible.
~ DUKE ELLINGTON

Most of the news I care about is summarized in the "Crime Watch" section of the local paper—little one-paragraph mentions of petty and unsolvable crimes that were reported to the Maui police.* Let somebody else turn to the sports page or drive up his blood pressure stewing over conditions in Haiti or North America or other islands.

Let somebody else study the comparables in the real estate classifieds, cussing under her breath. Give the comics to Junior; I can't understand them anymore.

I'd rather read about jimmied locks, rifled fannypacks, and hijacked roosters. When I brush against these stories, I feel most tormented by our common humanity and most aware of the need to commit wholesome, safe, and relatively harmless crimes.

As a writer I like "Crime Watch" because each paragraph tells a story about us. And so little of the story is told that I can freely imagine all the good parts—the why, the faces, the aftermath.

A woman in Kihei saw a man remove a screen and sneak into her kitchen. This was just after dawn. The man stole two wieners valued at sixty-nine cents. He snuck away.

So it says in "Crime Watch."

Now, this interests me. Why the hot dogs? Why not the kim chee or the smoked octopus? Do wieners make the perfect breakfast food? Or was the thief a kind of poet, acting out the muffled

* Shortly after I first published this essay, the local paper ceased running its "Crime Watch" feature. Was it something I said?

61

sexiness of the personal violation called "breaking and entering?" Why not take ALL the wieners? And how much time, I wonder, did the police officer spend calculating the true market value of a single pair of wieners? And why did the woman who reported this theft watch it transpire without intervening?

My mind races to fill in the details, but I must hold myself back. After all, both the wiener thief and the victim might be reading this article right now. My imagining has no right to cancel their fact.

In Kahului, a homeless woman left her purse in a phone booth. When she came back, all that she had—fifteen dollars—was gone.

I have been that down.

Once, when I was young and naïve, I offered a man a ride in my old rusty Volkswagen bug, and that man pulled a knife on me, stealing everything I had. I think he got four dollars and seventy-three cents, mostly in coins. What I remember most of all is the shaking of my knees, because I wasn't used to the idea of getting carved up with a knife.

That wouldn't happen now. Not the knees. Not the Volkswagen. Not even the ride.

The two previously mentioned "Crime Watch" stories came from Kihei and Kahului. Normally though when I read "Crime Watch," I go right away to my own geographical area. I hate to admit this, but it's true: the farther away the crime, the less I care. I always read "East Maui" and "Upcountry" first.

My neighborhood has its own big crimes. In fact, this statement is true of all neighborhoods: by its crimes shall you know it.

For instance, a Haʻiku man reported that his mailbox sustained twenty-five dollars in damages "from an unknown instrument"—not, I assume, a clarinet. In a related story, a pasture gate right down the street from my house was struck by a car.

In my neighborhood most of the big stories have to do with

the destruction of inanimate objects.

In Ha'iku, people like to break things, especially things made of metal. Especially mailboxes, cars, and guardrails. Especially after midnight, when Upcountry roads become insane bowling alleys, tires screaming and explosions of metal and glass. The happy, wild, loony nature of my neighbors makes itself obvious then. In the quiet night, I hear gleeful bursts of destruction, like fireworks—CRASH. KABLOOWEE. Wild laughter.

I understand this. Something inside of us just hates driving carefully all the time, paying car payments for five years, checking the oil, watching for little paint dings with their tell-tale streaks of rust. Most of us never once get the chance to drive the thing right into a wall at eighty miles an hour then stagger away from the wreck, shaken and drenched with sweat, fully alive, totally free, taking orders directly from God almighty himself.

For excitement this kind of physical challenge must be second only to birth. I've seen such acts of daring take place many times right in front of my house.

Too bad they cost so much.

Passionate spendthrifts, however, abound in my community, and the hubcaps, red glass, bent bumpers, and broken mirrors along the roadside speak not so much of simple destruction as of crazy yearning and the desire for transformation.

When I read my "Crime Watch," I look for the small but extravagant outbursts that characterize my people. Also, when I'm at my best, I sometimes remember to notice what's not there.

There are crimes that I never see in "Crime Watch."

My brother bought a house in Los Angeles several years ago. Now he and his wife have to explain to their children why they hear gunshots every night. I know a man who moved here from another part of that city only four months ago. He loved what he was doing over there. But he moved so that his son would be able to play in the front yard.

"I had a chain link fence and two hundred-pound dogs," he

said. "It wasn't enough."

For the Chinese this is the Year of the Dog. Citizens of Beijing, however, are not allowed to own dogs. In a park north of the city, citizens can rent a dog that they can walk. The price: twenty-three cents for ten minutes.

In April, Feng Quantang filed a lawsuit in Shenyang, China, asking for damages from the government because inspectors allegedly beat his illegal dog to death in front of him.

When I'm at my best, I remember some of the many crimes that we don't have to watch for.

India and Pakistan have been at war for the past nine years in a border dispute over the Siachen Glacier. No one can live on that glacier, yet the soldiers are shooting each other. For every soldier who gets shot, nine die from the blinding blizzards, the treacherous footing on ice-encrusted peaks, and wind-chilled temperatures of more than one hundred fifty degrees below zero.

No one from Ha'iku has volunteered to fight the noble battles of Siachen Glacier. This fact explains one of the many reasons I am happy to be here.

Mailboxes have it tough. For people, though—it's better than impossible.

Exquisite reasons
for ordinary acts: driving

Exquisite reasons
for ordinary acts: driving

They say that the odds of an average person getting attacked by a shark are one in several million. The odds of getting hit by lightning on any given day are one in two hundred and fifty million.

But these are not the statistics that changed Melvin Tanaka's life.

Melvin was sitting in his car waiting for his grandfather to come tottering out from Pukalani Superette with breakfast—six Spam musubi and two cans of Fanta. Somebody had left a copy of *Reader's Digest* in his car, so he was flipping through it and then he found this list of interesting statistics.

He found out that the odds of losing your virginity between the months of March and August are nearly one in ten. ("Did I...?" Melvin asked himself, but he couldn't remember.) And if you think you've seen a flying saucer, join ten percent of Americans. ("Never did," thought Melvin. Being a practical kind of guy, he added, "And I never going see one, too.")

But none of these statistics would make a person want to drive with insane slowness.

Then he read the odds for dying in a car crash—one in a hundred twenty-five. Car travel is ten times more dangerous than flying and twenty-five times riskier than taking the bus.

Still he didn't think too much about it. (That's the risk you take he thought.)

But then he found out the fact. The terrible fact. Certain cars are more dangerous than others said the article. And it listed the high-risk cars. It listed all the cars that Melvin loved. Corvettes and Camaros. Firebirds and Fieros.

Folks who drive those-kind cars face a one-in-thirty chance of death in a crash.

He blinked and looked again. Yes, the chance that he, Melvin, could die in the crash of a Nissan 300ZX is one in thirty!

One in thirty!

("That's like one day out of a month," he thought. "That's like one day in every month some guy's going come jumping up from out of the bushes and start shooting, li' dat. At me!") Melvin felt as though someone had just hit him in the chest with a dead ahi.

Melvin Tanaka happened to *drive* a Nissan 300ZX.

He has driven it very slowly. Ever since that day.

After he helped his grandfather wobble down into the car seat, Melvin pulled out of the Pook-Soop parking lot thinking hard. He wondered if he would still be alive enough to eat Spam musubi when he was eighty-two years old like his grandfather. And then, crossing the Pukalani bypass, he almost got clipped on the back fender by a Volvo coming down from Kula. "Slow down," he shouted.

He drove to Makawao at twenty miles per hour. It felt good.

I'll tell you. Melvin Tanaka is one hard-headed guy. When he decides to drive slow, he drives *very* slow. He don't care about nobody else.

He and his charcoal-gray Nissan 300ZX will never exceed the speed limit. Not any more. "If it's a risk, it's stupid"—that's Melvin's motto now.

And Melvin's not alone. When he snapped like that and made up his mind to "go the limit," he joined approximately one-fourth of the drivers who pass through the Upcountry town of Makawao.

He has even gone so far as to write a letter to the editor of a certain local newspaper. He even had a bumper sticker made that says this:

"Dare For Drive Slow."

You can spot Melvin everywhere he goes. He always has

five cars behind him, or seven, or nine. The cars are all nearly touching bumpers. And they're all driving like Melvin: slow.

You can see the tight lips and the frowns on the drivers' faces. You see lips moving, forming hostile words. Drivers lean their heads out the window and stare, trying to concentrate so hard that their stink-eye will turn into a laser death-ray and blow Melvin's Nissan right off the road.

Behind him you can see a convertible Beamer, a rented Tracker, then a backhoe. Even a backhoe is faster than Melvin Tanaka.

After that comes a higher-consciousness Datsun, its rusty parts held together with bumper stickers, road grime, and good will. (Miracles Happen!)

Then comes pounding a huge-tired, jewel-blue truck full of large Polynesian men. You can hear them yelling back there.

And up in front, Melvin. Cruising. Got his dark shades on. Got his rear-view mirror cranked to the side so he doesn't have to look behind. He's got plenty of time. He left the house thirty minutes early.

Melvin is the leader. He has formed a community.

Why don't they pass him, you ask? Why, you're obviously a stranger to these regions. The rest of America may be scrambling to find an on-ramp to the digital world traffic jam, but our rumpled district is filled with two-lane, shoulderless strands of asphalt spaghetti, some of them with hairpins so tight that you can drop your cigar out the window at the top of the curve then catch it again yourself as you're straightening out.

We have just about as much experience on four lane highways as we have with making snowmen.* In Upcountry Maui you don't pass. You gather.

Here you can't move out onto the

* Since that sentence was first published, miles one through seven of Haleakala Highway grew to four lanes. So now we have one stretch of road where drivers can slalom and maneuver to try to be the first ones to reach the same red light at approximately the same time.

street without having relationships of all kinds. The streets make us meet each other, and the rules of the road are deeply ingrained in the way we treat each other. And here is one of the most unbreakable rules of the road where I live: Every day, to one degree or another, the slowest person sets the pace.

Laugh if you want, but it seems to me that Melvin's chain-gang of traffic—going down Kaupakalua Road like a bobsled team on slow replay—that this is a perfect symbol for our times. This is what it means to live in a democracy.

In a democracy, all of us are equal. Equally slow.

The leaders get in front because everyone else is too swift to bother with the job. The leaders are always too cautious or too incompetent to keep up with the pace and too selfish to pull over and get out of the way.

The swift, of course, have it bad in a democracy. People with fire in their blood are always stuck in the back, frustrated, angry. And most people are jammed in the middle, feeling pressure from both front and back. Checking their watches.

It's democracy, I tell you, same as in Washington DC. In front we have our US Senate. In the rear we see America's city skies, punctuated with gunfire. The rest of us here in the middle, we have newspapers and pharmaceuticals.

The only question is: how do you feel about your place in the rhumba line?

Melvin liked his.

After six months of slowness, he was starting to get a swelled head. He liked being in charge, setting the pace for everyone. His friends got mad at him. "Brah," they said, "the speed limit means don't go SLOWER than that!" He ignored them.

Then, one day, it happened. He was coming around a curve with a dozen cars behind when suddenly he had to step on the brake. Someone was in front of him!

In a white Nissan 300ZX. Going twice as slow! When the car went around curves, the driver put on her blinkers.

She was pretty, she was young, and she was singing as she

drove. Melvin got one good look at her (on a hairpin turn), and his heart started to pound. A blowhole of love geysered in his chest. When after a mile or so she pulled off the road to visit with a newborn foal in a thick green pasture, Melvin did too.

The traffic whizzed by. Few people noticed the two strangers, hands on the fence, standing side-by-side looking at the baby horse, a rainbow arching over the pasture.

No one knows what the odds are for falling in love while driving a Nissan 300ZX. But at that time of year, the odds of seeing a rainbow on Kaupakalua Road on any given day are the best there can be.

One in one.

☽

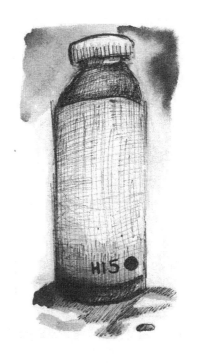

If you can't take this one, fine.
I don't wanna know.

If you can't take this one, fine.
I don't wanna know.

I'm forcing myself to write this. I can barely squeeze the words out. My shoulders are bunched up so tight I feel as if my neck is one big turnbuckle twisting tighter and tighter, and I keep panting and muttering, and every once in a while I jump out of my chair to go somewhere but there's nowhere to go, and my editor Carla's going to kill me if I don't get this thing done.

The problem is my topic. Stay with me now. I guarantee you'll be struck with the desire to stop reading as soon as I tell you. But don't you dare.

I'm writing about re…

re…re…re…

That re…thing.

You know, that thing where you take all that rubbish and all that poopoo kind stuff and instead of just throwing it out shazam like you're the king of the universe or something, instead of that you take each piece and look at it again and wash it off or peel off the label and put it in little bags or boxes, all sorted out like you're saving it all for some kind of weird museum, the family poop museum.

Recycling!

I'll tell you right now. I don't want to write about it, and I don't want to do it. "Don't play with your poopoo!" That's what my dad taught me.

My dad also taught me that bow ties are cool, that Walt Disney makes the only movies worth watching, and that I'd be handicapped all my life if I didn't know how to use a slide rule.

Dad was right. Then. I'm telling you. Those were the good old days.

And let me remind you of some other good old days. How about the Makawao dump, folks? Man, I used to love the Makawao dump—or the Makani "landfill" as it was officially called, although I'd rather call it a dump.

'Cause that's what we used to do. Dump. You and me. We'd throw anything in the back of the truck. Everything. Dirt. Plywood. Drywall. Used oil filters. Dead dryers. Dead cats. Dead TVs. Dead anything. Just drive up, dump, drive away. Cool.

But if you call it a "landfill," you can't have as much fun. Use that name and you have to remember that you have filled the land.

You can drive away. You can think about other things. But your dead poop remains.

And you and I pay to own that poop-filled land! It costs us six to seven *million dollars* to create one fifteen-acre working dump. And one of those might last for, oh, three years at the rate we're dumping. And then a skin of dirt goes over it all. And then for thirty years—yes, I said thirty—we, our kids, pay even more money to have the rotten place monitored by skilled professionals who look for leachate (stuffs that drip down) and sniff for methane (stinks that drift up).

So thirty years from now when I'm a rotten old geezer, people on Maui will be paying top dollar so that some expert can baby-sit my useless old poop.

I remember my last trip to the dear old dump, where the wind blew grit in our teeth and the white egrets would rise up out of the stench whenever the earth quaked under the weight of the back-beeping earthmoving metal disasters that were tearing the land apart.

May 2, 1992. I know that date. It was the exact day after the Makani land... after the dump had closed forever and without my permission.

That day for some reason, in the innocence of my stupidity, I loaded my truck—a white, rotting old V-8 Chevy three-quarter-ton pickup—to the point where I was pretty sure I wouldn't get a ticket but, though I wouldn't admit it to you or anyone, I wasn't really sure.

Not totally.

In that load that day, you could sense some bad stuff. There were petroleum products on the move. There were organics slowly stirring back to life—only this time in a different form. There were steel beds and file cabinets, two apartment-sized washing machines. Instant fossils.

I was like the *Exxon Valdes* pushing itself up Kaupakalua Road on bald tires.

And then I reached the locked gate at the former dump. A pitiless sign informed me that this was now a former "landfill" and our Makani "landfilling" privileges had been revoked forever. Blown away with the "makani," the winds of change.

As my Portuguese neighbor had warned me that one day, about a year before, when I'd been up there sweeping the last bit of "fill" from back of the *Chevron Valdez*—the haoles had finally managed to fill up the dump.

So I headed off to the next closest dump, to the Kahului dump, saying wild and crazy things to myself in the cab of the truck, the load swaying with lots of sloshing and grinding, the gas gauge shaking down near the E. I got there all right, but I got there five minutes after they closed, and then I headed back Upcountry, not sure what fate lay ahead for *Moby Poop*.

The tire blew two miles up the Haleakala Highway.

Rush hour traffic screamed past like a fellow lunatic spitting tar hail into my face. I shoved the jack under that pile of you-know-what and went to work. I remember lying underneath that cargo while the whole thing depended on the tilted spindle of the slender jack, and every time a car ripped past (every three seconds on average) the darkness above shook and moaned.

The spare tire was low on air, but I thought it might hold. I knew I was lucky to find a spare at all.

Soon it started to rain, and I believe it started to rain just as, one mile farther up the highway, an engine rod kicked through the crankcase of that truck, and hot motor oil shot like heart's blood across what was suddenly an expensive piece of clever, though somewhat rusted, scrap metal.

As I stood there, half-paralyzed, leaning face-first against the side of my garbage pile, I couldn't imagine how I was going to get five tons of trash off of the side of the main highway of the most beautiful island on planet Earth.

At one point I glanced all about me and saw sunshine and blue skies on every horizon, wherever I turned. The rain was dumping on me, only on me. Only on me and on my friend, the ride of Frankenstein. The rain was dumping.

Dumping.

The new leachate was dripping onto my dirty broken Adidas. The new methane stench rose into the air.

Listen. Nearly two million tons of commodities get imported every year from North America to Kahului Harbor. Two hundred thousand tons of these commodities, trashed, get stuffed every year into the Kahului landfill. The Kahului landfill will overflow by the year 2026.

My old truck held only a ton of that industrialized shit.

We live on a small island and we drink water that soaks through this small sponge of rock. We eat the food of this land, or at least we can when we can find it.

This land has swallowed so much. Its lips have been pried open with shovels. And the land has made good of what we've given it, and the land pushes us upright, pushes us to attention.

When I take a handful of soil and breathe in its messages, I know I am home. I can smell my own best self. Our best selves.

I know the land will grow toward what we plant. After all, what we plant is an investment.

We need street-side pick-up of every manufactured product that we can possibly send back to North America. Send it back when we're done with it.

Make an agreement. When things break down, we send

them back.

And hey, manufacturers, no need to pay us for the service. We'll accept the charges. We won't even complain when we have to go out and buy another washing machine or lawn mower or rake; we won't ask you why we should pay to replace your short-lived products.

If you live in Haʻiku, you never blame anybody for the fact that things rust, turn to compost, join the soil, become part of our lives—or else get shipped back to the pollution pits they came from. "Thank you, Mainland Soup Company, for the temporary use of your can." I would be happy to recycle if *that* was the game.

After all, the barges have to go back for their next shipments, so they might as well take the crapped-out products with them.

❧

Skinny-dipping can lead to other more serious crimes

Skinny-dipping can lead to other
more serious crimes

Parents, keep this article out of the hands of children.

It exposes a shameless crime, a crime our leaders have seen as threatening to the very fabric of Maui society—threatening, in fact, to fabrics of any kind.

I'm talking about skinny-dipping.

Here are the rude facts. It's Saturday, August fifth, and you're looking at the front page of *The Maui News*. A man and a woman have been arrested for swimming without their suits in a natural pool somewhere between Hana and Keʻanae.

You can picture the scene. The waterfall. Ginger plants. The police car. The stern officer with his gun, his fists planted on his fully-clothed hips, saying, "All right you two, come out with your hands up."

"Okay never mind that," he adds hastily. "Hands down is okay."

When the criminals appear in Makawao District Court, the judge blasts them: "I will not tolerate such actions!" He fines them fifty bucks each.

This fifty bucks (two times) is actually more money than you think. At the time that this crime occurs, the minimum wage is just one dollar forty an hour, which is less than one-fifth of the minimum today. That makes the fine more like two hundred or two hundred fifty bucks (two times).

The year is 1969.

Let me say it right now, because you're probably thinking it: Shame.

Shame. Shame. How could those people be so rude?

Most of us spend our entire lives trying not to look at each other's buns. And of course, the law protects our constitutional right not to look at buns. (I think that's covered in the Bill of Rights, along with our right to leave half-eaten boxes of popcorn on the floor of the movie theater after the show.)

And now here come these bad people, willfully creating a situation whereby innocent folks who are driving past might accidentally glance to the left and, without wanting it—AUWE!—glimpse those buns.

Okay. Now let's get to the interesting part. I want to know why *The Maui News* printed this story on the front page. I mean, front-page news is for catastrophes and disasters: "Haleakala Erupts!" or "President declares War on Drugs!"

Not, certainly, "Buns Bagged in Nahiku!"

Front-page placement suggests that all Maui people should alert themselves to this story. Other front-page stories from that year, 1969, include occasional reports on Maui boys dying in Vietnam.

On that same day, July fifth, you see two other lead stories somehow related to the nudism-threat piece above. In one, fourteen people at Makena Beach are arrested by the police vice squad on the morning of July third and sentenced to thirty days in jail. They have been trespassing. If they don't want to serve the thirty days, they can accept a plane ride back home. They can be banished from the kingdom.

The article calls these people "hippies."

The other lead story, same day, tells of the court cases awaiting the Peahi residents of "Banana Patch." The drop-out cruisers of Banana Patch have created a free-form, Gilligan's-Island village, and now they must face the authorities to answer charges of alleged violations of sanitary regulations, building and housing codes, and land-use codes.

It's clear to anyone who's scanning this newspaper that Maui has a terrible problem with hippies. In fact, the paper obviously ranks this public concern right up there with "Safe Boating Week To Be Observed Here."

Two weeks later, a new law makes hitchhiking illegal in Maui County. (It still is.)* This ban on hitching comes two days after "Moon Day"—so declared by Mayor Elmer Cravalho on the famous day of the "giant leap for all mankind."

The next June, an actual rock that was captured from the moon goes on public display down at War Memorial Gym. The rock, a trophy of conquest sent out to the border tribes to convince them that the central authority is really quite bad-ass, draws a big crowd. (Some of you were there I'm sure.) On Maui, the moon-rock viewing crowds are the largest in Hawai'i, larger even than on O'ahu—five thousand one hundred and seventy-two people lining up in a single day.

On that same day, Goro Hokama announces that he is seeking his ninth term on the County Council. He will win, and he will manage to keep his okole fixed to that important seat of leadership for another twenty-four years, right up to the last election.** (I mention this only to suggest that Maui County's style of leadership has not shifted significantly since the dire, community-poisoning events of 1969.)

And—here it is again. I'm still looking through the old papers, and right around Moon Day I find another nudie story. Six people get arrested for trespassing and for indecent exposure out at remote Honolua Bay on West Maui.

On the same day, a respected Up-country leader speaks of the forces of evil that have destroyed the nation's moral fiber. He addresses a Memorial Day ceremony at the Veteran's Cemetery on Baldwin Avenue. The valiant Maui men who are buried all around this orator (he tells us) urge him to proclaim to all who will hear: "You, the living, have failed us."

The speaker has eavesdropped on

* Since the original publication of this essay, the law against hitchhiking quietly disappeared. Who can afford to be a hippie anymore, anyway?

** Mr. Hokama has since retired. His son Mr. Hokama the younger now occupies the same throne in council chambers.

the mutterings of the mortal remains from the soil beneath his feet, but the newspaper article doesn't tell us what kind of weird telephone he has employed. It just tells us this: "We the living have failed to stop the false prophets."

And who are these false prophets destroying everything good and decent? This respected Makawao leader describes them poetically: "These modern pied pipers with their flutes pipe our youth down the indescribably evil and lonely roads of marijuana, heroin and the madness of LSD."

For over a year the paper has been emphasizing lots of little stories about indecent-exposure busts, long-haired trespassers, and Banana Patch hand-wringing, so we know who these pied pipers really are.

The hippies. They want our moon-rock.

Now we have what we needed, an effective group label. ("Hippie" works as well for this as Nigger, Moke, Pencil-Neck Jap, and so on.) The newspaper has popularized its version of the problem, and our leaders are making hateful, group-label speeches. Now we're ready for violence.

Next thing you see is a story titled "'Hippies Our Biggest Problem'—Williams." It quotes the president-elect of the West Maui Business Association as saying that the group's "single, most important task is 'to make Lahaina less attractive to the hippies.'"

No one bothers to define the term "hippie," but who cares? Everybody knows what they've done.

Mayor Cravalho makes a gloomy speech about some "organized, overt movement...for the total destruction of the system and establishment of which I am a part." He says that, "These people will try to exploit any cause, real or imagined, which can divide the community."

The Maui police freely admit to unconstitutional practice against anyone with long hair. For example, instead of issuing citations, the police routinely arrest and harass long-hairs for minor traffic violations. No one objects, except a few gooey-eyed lawyers fussing about civil liberties. Long-hair lawyers. Everybody knows what they want to do.

And then the big story breaks. The one every *Maui News* reader has been waiting for. June 27, 1970. Five hepatitis cases. Originating in the Banana Patch.

Maybe.

The authorities now have a reason to get in there and number all their bones.

You see a photo of the police chief, a Hawaiian man in a suit who converses with two bearded, white hoboes in ragged clothes. The two white men have their hands clasped over their groins, as if they are being arrested for skinny-dipping. They're telling the police chief that, vibrationally speaking, broccoli is higher on the chain to God than, say, an animal with a bad attitude, like an anteater for instance. The police chief is imagining kicking their suntanned buns onto a Navy cargo transporter that will drop them off in Barrow, Alaska.

By early August, cases of hepatitis and dysentery start cropping up around the island. Despite citizen protests that government sources are giving false information, the mayor, the Department of Health, and the newspaper make it clear that the hippies, all of them, have sickened the people of Maui.

No one asks why our public health safeguards are so inadequate that a single case of hepatitis can spread throughout the community. No. No one stops to say, "Now wait—if some poor Portuguese man got hepatitis, would we brand all Portuguese as enemies of the people?" No. The problem is simple. It's the hippies. And everyone knows a hippie just by looking.

So, on August 29 the first violence is reported. Innocent people using Kalama Park are beaten and chased off with machetes and revolvers. Tourists camping in the Kihei area are frightened away.

The attackers are termed "locals." The attacked, "hippies." No one questions what those terms mean.

Again let me say it. Shame on those rude people who dis-
regarded social customs and took off one-too-many articles of
clothing while conjuring up their banana-patch villages and
adam-and-eve frolics.

Notice, however, something else. Group hatred was sanc-
tioned in 1970 by the leaders of this community. The aloha
spirit grew sick. Of all the petty crimes of those years, this one
offends me most.

And that's the naked truth.

THE PAST

*Infectious diseases
made us what we are today*

Infectious diseases
made us what we are today

As King Kamehameha XXVI recently pointed out, the united territories of "The Aloha Bloc" now exert more influence on this planet than any political power in the recorded history of the human race.

It doesn't matter how you measure—in square miles, number of citizens, military advantage, wealth, or knowledge. No nation has ever come close to the present success of the Commonwealth of Greater Hawai'i.

Islam and China, our two rivals for world power today, have both grown slowly over long histories of cold-blooded empire building. But Greater Hawai'i, which includes the entire Pacific Basin, Australia, most of Southeast Asia, more than half of both North and South America, as well as colonies and small member nations in both Europe and southern Africa, has taken only two hundred years to grow to this size.

Two centuries ago, Hawai'i consisted of no more than eight hundred thousand souls living in total isolation from the rest of the world. At that time, the English (Hawai'i's "discoverers") were set on a course to dominate the world. Rich with their clever Industrial-Revolution toys and tools, they were exploring and capturing new lands all around the globe.

Of course, the idea of a "British Empire" seems ridiculous today. Here at the dawn of the twenty-first century England is just a depressed colony of Saudi Arabia. The small remaining population of native Brits is a textbook case of an oppressed aboriginal race—impoverished, illiterate, and malnourished. The English language may well be dying out.

For another example of a global "wannabe" that never was,

look at the backwards little United States. The thirteen colonies had already declared their independence from England two years before Captain Cook arrived in Hawai'i. It didn't take more than ten years to lay the foundations for a strong government designed along Greek and Roman models. They began to think about expanding westward.

Within fifty years, however, their government had all but collapsed. The will to expand, or even to resist invasion, seemed to abandon these newly invented people.

Today the US remains thirteen small, bickering colonies hemmed in by the vast, thriving Native American cultures, the thundering herds of bison, and the undamaged American wilderness which is protected and managed by the kahuna councils of the Hawaiian Commonwealth.

And how did these historical changes come about? What caused the collapse of the Western world and the meteoric rise of tiny Hawai'i to global prominence?

We like to think that these dramatic changes were caused by the natural superiority of the Hawaiian world-view. After all, the kapu system is just plain practical, logical, and humane. Of course we like it best.

And yet, other systems do have their merits. I know it's hard to imagine, but democracy, capitalism, communism, or some other philosophy could have come to dominate the world.

We tend to assume that Hawaiian spiritual practices offer the only truth, that other religions are confused and foolish. We're accustomed to the sight of our stone temples, our heiau, throughout the world. We're comfortable with the fact that our annual Makahiki festival is now a global tradition, even in Muslim and Buddhist lands.

In our bellies, though, we know better. We've been taught not to be so narrow-minded. We know that all religions are founded in truth. Any one of them (even Christianity!) could have come to dominate our lives.

People do not give up their beliefs lightly. Remember how

many Hawaiian missionaries were slaughtered by the frightened natives when they brought the good word to Christian nations in the Americas and Europe.

No. The Hawaiians dominate now—but not necessarily from any innate betterness. They dominate because of good luck. To put the matter bluntly, the early Hawaiians simply didn't die.

They had better immune systems than the English.

Hawai'i now rules the world because of a disease, a virus. The Last Laugh, they called it, though it was anything but funny.

Remember. When Captain Cook arrived in Hawai'i, his sailors brought diseases. Wherever Western people traveled, their diseases destroyed whole societies. Syphilis, smallpox, cholera, chicken pox, measles, and other fatal illnesses were wasting rival cultures.

In Peru, for example, nine million people welcomed the strange-looking white men. In less than fifty years, ninety-three percent of these people were dead. The few survivors could hardly resist the spread of Western culture.

The same collapse occurred even in Tahiti, where seventy-five percent of the people sickened and died over a twenty-five-year period.

People of the West believed that their success was being granted by God; in fact, it had been caused by germs.

The tables turned when Cook arrived in Hawai'i. Though he brought all the white diseases, none of them proved to be a wide-scale problem for people living in these islands. Kahuna still do not agree about the reason for this immunity.

Ironically, though, Cook's men contracted a disease in Hawai'i, a totally new disease to which they had absolutely no resistance. The Last Laugh.

Soon after his one visit to these islands, while heading onward to explore the Pacific Northwest, Cook observed several of his crewmembers falling prey to this strange new disease. As Cook's badly-spelled logbook says, "Theyr sides shaike, their faces contorting unto ungodly smiles, and they gaspe as if laughing, where unto they meet theyr oblivion and are dead."

The disease spread quickly among the crew, and nothing in the ship's infirmary could be found to prevent it, or even slow its shark-like attacks. Many of the healthy crew members abandoned their tasks and lay on the ship's deck, paralyzed with terror and waiting to die. Stunned, Cook chose to turn back for England. All along the route of that desperate flight, Cook's men chuckled their way into heaven. The dwindling crew abandoned one of their two ships in Tierra del Fuego, then made a mad dash to the Thames.

Cook himself howled to eternal rest near the coast of Spain.

In the end, only twenty-three crew members returned to the streets of London, and the rapid decline of Western culture can be measured in quick, hilarious blooms of death that spread outward from that moment in London to Europe and to all its creations.

Let's be brutally honest. Suppose one-tenth of the people you know suddenly die. It's a shock. Everyone's rattled, anxiety-ridden. You would find yourself at the heiau more often, making sacrifices for one reason or another. But suppose things get worse. Suppose, ten years later, nine out of every ten people you know have vanished in agony (including all your kahuna). You wouldn't believe it. In fact, you wouldn't believe anything. Disbelief would flood every crevice of your life. Faith would dart like a desperate rabbit for any hole or shade or shelter.

With every death, you lose some portion of your spirit. When ninety-three percent die, then only seven percent of your faith remains.

If Hawai'i had lost even half that number of its people, then we might be living today in islands dominated by Western traditions and government. The native people here might be just as demoralized and frightened as the pathetic Brits are today in England.

Life could have been far different.

Let's not forget that any spot on the human earth has the

potential to become the attention of the world, a source of great ideas, the belly-button of our species.

I know this sounds far-fetched, but depressed little towns like London or even the miserable shacks of Manhattan all have this potential. With luck, they too could have attained the glory of a place such as magnificent Makawao, which is today truly the "center of the universe."

Kamehameha's trade, white trash,
and the Taro Festival

Kamehameha's trade, white trash, and the Taro Festival

It's spring of 1994, and American troops are pulling out of Somalia taking with them their motorized and electronic gadgets and their supply streams of Corn Flakes, Pop Tarts, paper towels, nudie magazines, disposable razors, Spam, microwave popcorn, raspberry jam, pocket calculators, pump-action toothpaste dispensers, Ray-Bans, and Snoop Doggy Dogg CDs. To be more precise, all *white* soldiers are leaving. (Europeans, Canadians, like that.) The remaining UN troops come from third-world countries, and their trash is worth almost nothing.

For the past couple of years, thousands of Somalians found prosperity by "redistributing" the contents of the white soldiers' dumpsters. The rubbish of white officers, in particular, has turned quite a few locals into Mogadishan millionaires. Now, as politics shift and troops go, the black-market white trash industry is collapsing.

Only white people toss out valuable rubbish.

(Please forgive me for equating first-world countries with "white people." US troops, for example, contain people of all colors of course, so here's yet another example of a stupid group label. However, I am simply using the terminology of the Somali trash merchants themselves, who rate their garbage sources "white" when they mean, as I do, the culture dominated by pink-colored men.)

I heard about the trash merchants of Mogadishu by listening to public radio. That was on Monday morning. I'd just come back from Hana and the second annual Taro Festival. The coincidence got me thinking about our own history and the fact that, even though we ourselves come and go, our trash remains and leaves its mark on the generations that follow.

It's safe to imagine that no African man will ever feel quite the same about local politics after eating a blueberry Pop-Tart while staring at a nearly naked picture of Cindy Crawford. The same change happened here, too, in 1778 when white people's trash dropped like a bomb into Hawaiian culture.

Not that Captain Cook had a lot of trash. He certainly wasn't setting up dumpsters on every new shore. His men weren't hurling onto the reefs bulging Steel Sacks full of empty beer bottles and broken toasters. No. But the Hawaiians did find a great, culture-rocking wonderment in Cook's few remainders.

Nails, for example.

Nails were the first haole trash items, and the locals traded pigs and sweet potatoes for them. If you are good at pounding and shaping stones (and the Hawaiians were very good at that) you can easily pound a nail into a knife.

Cook sighted the island of Kaua'i first, and he brought his two ships close to the coast near Waimea. There in a scuffle over nails a Hawaiian was given instead a different little piece of metal—a ball shot from a gun. Of the countless Hawaiian deaths brought about by white trash, this was the first.

I've taken this information from *The Life of Captain James Cook*, a big, fat door-stop of a book written in the early 1970s by J. C. Beaglehole. Beaglehole tells all, and I've picked through the stories to find out exactly what trash the good discoverer and his crew left behind.

The seas were rough off Kaua'i that day. Looking for shaky anchorage, the *Resolution* and the *Discovery* crept around to the west shore of Ni'ihau. They needed fresh water. A landing party led by Cook's first lieutenant, a chap named John Gore, was sent to Ni'ihau. Then a storm blew in, and the white men were forced to stay on shore for two nights.

This group dropped off another significant piece of Western trash—a sexually transmitted disease called syphilis.

To Cook's credit, he was upset about this particularly dev-astating deposit. It was, he wrote, "the very thing...that I had above all others wished to prevent." He had refused to let his men stay overnight on shore, but the storm thwarted his will. Just like you and me, he meant well.

Clerke, captain of the *Discovery*, blamed it all on their white-trash crew. "Our Seamen are in these matters so infernal and dissolute a Crewe that for the gratification of the present pas-sion that affects them they would entail universal destruction upon the whole of the Human Species."

A nail, a bullet, and the love-killing disease. Cook and his folks took little in exchange—water and food staples. They gave the Niihauans some goats, pigs, and seeds "of the English breed," none of which survived the next year. Discouraged by continued stormy weather, the white folks then set off for the Bering Sea.

Nine months later, Cook returned from Alaska, and he spot-ted Haleakala first. He "lay to" along our North Shore. (The first European to see Ho'okipa!) Then he let the current carry him against the trade winds along the coast toward Hana. He had in mind rounding the eastern end of Maui to seek shelter on our leeward coast. One sight of the Big Island, though, con-vinced him to cross the channel.

If not for that decision, he might have landed in Kaupo or Kahikinui, where huge populations of Maui people fished, grew sweet potatoes, and managed the vital shipping traffic passing back and forth along that now ghostly and ecologically devastated stretch of this island. Instead, he brought his trash to Kealakekua Bay.

And there begins modern Hawaiian history.

On Hawai'i the Englishmen gave whatever they felt they could give in exchange for the heaps of supplies that the Hawaiians were letting them take—which included the entire fence surrounding the heiau at Kelakeakua along with most of its carved-wood ki'i or god-images. The English needed firewood.

In exchange, Cook had his blacksmith fashion a little metal toolbox as a gift for the great chief Kalaniopu'u.

When an old white seaman named Will Watman died of a stroke, they buried his body at the foot of the heiau and nailed up a little sign. Metal nails wouldn't have lasted any longer than a roadside mirror on a Ha'iku curve. (The one put up by the county next to my house: forty-five minutes.) So out of respect for the old seaman, the white people used wooden pegs instead.

These were fine gifts, I suppose, but the Hawaiians wanted more. They lost patience with the fundamental stinginess of these first tourists. To make things fair, the locals started popping out nails wherever they could get them, even out of the ships themselves. The English considered this activity to be "theft."

(By contrast, Cook and his men were just "borrowing.")

Bad feelings escalated until Cook himself fired a rifle into the chest of a chief. Then in return he received a fatal stabbing to the neck. Cook was slain with a piece of his own trash, an iron dagger.

Cook's bones and hands were buried at sea, the great chief Kalaniopu'u was given a quality British red felt cloak in exchange for his own cloak that women had exquisitely handcrafted from feathers, and Clerke ordered the surviving crews to sail away for good.

Now here is a curious fact. Three days before Captain Cook was mortally stabbed with an iron dagger, this same Lieutenant Clerke struck a deal with a quiet but seriously ambitious young chief. No doubt Clerke felt that this young chief, who had sailed with him on the excruciating crossing from Ke'anae Maui to Kealakekua, promised to be an ally of promise. The kind of strongman you could sign a treaty with. Why else would Clerke have accepted the chief's odd cape of feathers in exchange for a real prize—a set of nine long iron daggers.

That young chief was Kamehameha. I wonder what he did with those daggers.

Kamehameha was the Mogadishan millionaire of his time. He later took possession of a ship's cannon then kidnapped two sailors who knew how to shoot the thing. With that cannon he was able to blast the warriors of Maui back into 'Iao Valley in desperate and bloody defeat. Then he moved on to O'ahu and sovereignty. He eventually retired next to his two-story warehouse packed with fine fabrics and uniform jackets and hand mirrors and rifles.

Western trash had a holy allure for Kamehameha, but don't kid yourself that we are any less naïve. In fact, Kamehameha's trade defines the rest of our history. It begins with nine long daggers and escalates to include the tons of metal rubbish and unexploded ordnance that litter Kaho'olawe, the I-beams in our tall buildings, the nuclear subs that visit.

The Hana Taro Festival looked to me like the celebration that Captain Cook interrupted when he sailed into Kealakekua Bay. In Hana I have met young taro farmers, forward-thing, beautiful people. If I'd offered them nine long daggers, or partnerships in a hardware store, or high-level positions in a new resort, they would have said no.

For some reason we are now ready to make a choice that's different from Kamehameha's trade. I feel bad for the folks in Somalia. They may be facing two hundred years of cloudy confusion as they sort through the garbage. But in Hana, Sunday, the sun shone. It was a beautiful day.

☾

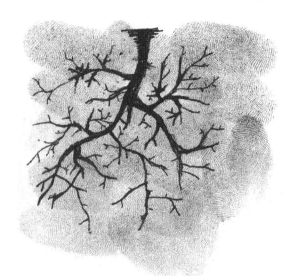

My feet keep imagining the
rocks beneath the mud

My feet keep imagining
the rocks beneath the mud

My older brother is deformed.

I was told to take care of him and keep the family together, and he would make sure that I would never go hungry. It bothers me to admit, though, that I haven't given him much attention lately.

His name is Kalo. He hangs out with the folks in Keʻanae and Wailuanui.* When I drive to Hana, I stop at the overlook and see him down there. He looks happy enough, I guess. Putting on a brave face.

I'm talking about the taro plant, of course.

You may not buy the "brother" story because it's not scientific, but I think science has its limits and I'll stick with the version passed along by the Hawaiians.

Unless the two brothers stick together, they say, the light of Hawaiʻi will fade to black.

No resort development will ever get it lit again. They can pour concrete over the kalo landscape. They can build a Grand Blatant Resort Keʻanae, with a gigantic bronze kalo plant sculpture on either side of the porte

★ These are side-by-side coastal districts on Haleakalaʻs windward shoreline located about midway on the road between Hana and the known world. People call this area the Koʻolau because it lies at the mouth of the great Koʻolau Gap, which swoops down from Haleakala Crater. Formerly one of richest food-producing areas in the Hawaiian Islands, the Koʻolau is now almost unpopulated. Many of the old kalo ponds are weedy and fallow. The productive ones suffer for lack of streamwater, which is largely diverted for use elsewhere. Hawaiian culture is the only human culture on Earth that discovered how to rely on kalo as its staple food, and it's the only one that pounded kalo into a nutritious goop called poi.

These days, according to a study published by the University of Hawai'i's College of Tropical Agriculture and Human Resources, fewer than five percent of the people of Hawai'i eat poi as a staple.

cochere.

The county can pass laws preserving Hawai'i, but there will be nothing spiritual left to preserve unless you and I take care of the family.

So they say.

Now when I stand on the Hana road gazing down at those fanned-out lava peninsulas that butt into the thundering surf and find myself staring at all the lo'i, the squared-edged artificial marshes continuously flooded with cool mountain water and fattening with the flag-like rich green leaves of the kalo, I think about these things.

How ironic that we get to stop our cars there and stare down at the old fields and the few people who still keep the old covenant. Why do we stare?

It's not just how pretty it all looks. We stare as if we're straining to understand an urgently yelled message in a foreign tongue. We are deaf. We see the lips move, but we can't quite hear.

And you people down there, the ones we're looking at, poor folks, you can't even take a leak in the back yard without the risk of being captured forever in the home video of honeymooners from Indiana.

I'm sure you'd rather be left alone. But you won't be. In 1927, prison laborers cut the "belt road" through, connecting Ke'anae with the real world. Now you can drive to Burger King in little more than an hour.

Every day people stop and stare. They can see what you've got. You're not safe.

Nosy people like me write about you, pass along the hearsay. For example, when you work in the muddy lo'i of Ke'anae, your feet work down to the bottom and you can feel the bony tips of the 'a'a, the rough lava, underneath. So they say.

I haven't been able to get that idea out of my feet.

Have I lost a brother?

I never see him anywhere but with you. He used to be everywhere on Maui. Everybody was his friend. I hear he gets over to the west side now and then, out by Honokohau, and he's got friends in Waihe'e and Waikapu. That's about it these days.

Never comes Upcountry anymore.

Mom and Dad made a baby, called him Haloa. But he was funny looking. He turned into a kalo plant. They had a second kid, called him Haloa, too. He was funny looking in a different way. Turned into a human being.

Mom said, "You two ugly boys better stick together, malama, take care of each other. 'Cause if you don't, I don't know who's gonna!"

So the two brothers traveled around the Pacific Ocean taking care of each other. Life was good. So they say.

Kalo, the older one, used example to teach his ignorant little brother how to live. He grew all his offspring, his 'oha, the smaller copies of himself, all around the main stalk, as many as five generations of copies of himself. All these 'oha together, that's the 'ohana, the family.

When the family breaks up, that's good. The kids get out from under the parent's shadow. Nothing is lost. Everything is magnified. This is the family story.

The saying goes: I maika'i no ke kalo I ka 'oha. Judge the goodness of the taro by looking at the sprouts. You learn a lot about the family by looking at the kids.

In Hawai'i, the two brothers got along better than anywhere else on the planet. One square mile of Hawaiian-style lo'i can feed as many as fifteen thousand people. The Hawaiians grew three hundred kinds of kalo, grew it anywhere there was water—in the windward valleys, on rock and beach flats near stream systems, on leeward slopes that cupped even a little moisture, even in mulch pits that they created on lava fields.

About five hundred years ago plenty of kalo was grown in the now-jungle hills above Ke'anae peninsula but the peninsula itself was barren. The farmers used to come down to the flat lava platform to fish and gather 'opihi and limu.

Their ali'i or headman didn't want to leave well enough alone. He was caught up in a rivalry with the headman of the next district, Wailua. He wanted to challenge the kalo supremacy of Wailuanui. So he talked his people into carrying dirt down from the hills, flattening and covering the 'a'a flow on the peninsula. Gradually they built up the soil, formed the walls and irrigation ways that you now see from the lookout on the Hana road. They turned a sheet of solid rock into a beautiful watery garden district.

Wars raged in this area, bloody fighting between Big Island fighters and Maui defenders. During the fourteenth century a huge war fleet landed here, and the warriors doubled back on foot to ambush the Maui troops in Hana. But no one ever messed with the people of Ke'anae and Wailuanui.

No one was ever stupid enough to do damage to older brother.

In 1778 Captain Cook anchored the *Resolution* right off the shores of Wailua. Kamehameha, not yet the conqueror of all Hawai'i, went out from Wailua shore and spent the night on Cook's ship. This is still our history. It happened here.

Ever since the Hawaiians created those lo'i, hundreds and hundreds of generations of 'oha have been snapped off and replanted. Born again. The plants that waggle their green flags across the Ke'anae peninsula today must be, in fact, the very same plants that those clever farmers and water engineers brought down to the peninsula centuries ago. These are the same fields. This is the same earth that they carried. Gesture of planting the same. Harvest habit the same. The same life.

Kalo is to the Hawaiians what the buffalo is to the Lakota Sioux, what corn is to the Hopi, the acorn to the Pomo, reindeer to the Laplanders, and (I suppose) the drive-thru burger to Americans.

The everything symbol. The sine qua non. The without-which-there-is-nothing.

Is there any purpose to kalo anymore now that we have instant mashed potatoes? Have cattle replaced the need for the buffalo? Does a white leghorn do for the phoenix?

You learn a lot about the family by looking at the kids.

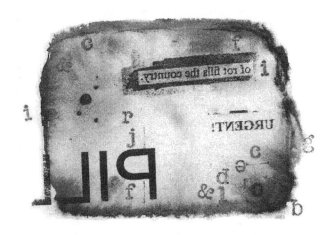

A string of newspaper stories
I'd dearly love to read

A string of newspaper stories
I'd dearly love to read

First one. Monday's paper.

Weirdness in Hana
Cop Vanishes
Has Ka'ahumanu Returned?

Sightings of the ghost of Hawai'i's former ruling chiefess Ka'ahumanu had tongues wagging in Hana on Sunday morning. Rumors spoke of mysterious flashing lights on Hana Bay and the strange disappearance of two people, one of them a police officer.

No official explanation has been offered for the unusual events, reported by several witnesses.

Police and civilian search parties have scoured the greater Hana area since dawn hoping to locate the missing policeman and a Paukukalo teenager.

"We search this way out past 'Oheo," said Hana fisherman Abe Nakabuchi. "Then we search that way almost to Ke'anae. Never find nothin."

The missing officer, whose name was not released, was last seen at the eastern end of Hana Bay around 12:30 am Saturday. Unexplained lights apparently coming from the back side of Kauiki Head had drawn a small, late-night crowd of the curious. The on-duty policeman was responding to calls of alarm about the lights.

"These lights were bright, man," said one witness, a ceramist from Idaho visiting the Hana area. "Like fireworks, only you couldn't see where they were coming from. I still don't know what was going down."

The policeman was last seen walking into the darkness on a cinder footpath that rounds the eastern end of the bay.

Another witness, a lobster fisherman from Nahiku, said, "He ask us what's happening here. So I tell him. Those lights coming from Ka'ahumanu cave. Had to be. So he go. He stay going around the pu'u. Then right where that cave is, boom. Drums start up. Hawaiian style. Loud."

Another witness said, "Get chicken skin just talking about it."

At about the same time, seventeen-year-old Deeanne Pejoria jumped from the truck where she had been parked along with three other teenagers. Witnesses say that she ran up the trail impulsively, ignoring the cries of her friends.

One of the friends, Rudybellinda Kipikipihiwi said, "Then everything got real quiet. Even I stopped screaming. We could hear a voice, but we never catch the words."

Pejoria never returned.

Authorities may be baffled, but local residents express no doubts that these events mark the return of Hana's most famous former citizen.

Ka'ahumanu, the favored wife of Kamehameha I, governed the kingdom of Hawai'i from 1819 to 1832. She dismantled the kapu system, the rules and regulations through which the ruling chiefs expressed their power. When the missionaries arrived one year later, Ka'ahumanu set the stage for modern Hawai'i by publicly embracing Christianity.

She was born a refugee of war in a cave on Kauiki Head, the cinder hill that forms the right flank of Hana Bay. A brass plaque marks the spot.

"Some of us has spoke wit' her," said one local resident who did not want to be named. "She says she changing her mind now. She wen' make a mistake, one big friggin' mistake. Back then, she'd like us learn all the haole ways. So, how much did we learn? Choke I tell you. Enough already."

Second one. Tuesday's paper.

Alleged Ka'ahumanu Hijacks Mall
Liberty House Becomes Battleground

A woman posing as the former Hawaiian queen Ka'ahumanu succeeded in driving the customers and employees out of Ka'ahumanu Shopping Center and into the parking lots yesterday afternoon. She and her followers then seized control of the Liberty House department store.*

Police have cordoned off the entire shopping center and are attempting to negotiate the surrender of the woman claiming to have returned from the dead.

"I don't think she's planning to come out," said police spokesman Detective Hercules Silva. "She's saying that this is her Center. She's placed a kapu on all the stores."

The self-proclaimed Ka'ahumanu arrived at Ka'ahumanu Center without warning at about ten a.m. accompanied by an estimated thirty to forty followers, at least a dozen of whom are muscular "warriors" bearing authentic-looking ancient Hawaiian spears and clubs.

Frightening the customers with harmless but vivid flashes of light and threatening gestures, she and her followers managed to clear the Center within fifteen minutes. No one was hurt, and no buildings were damaged.

Thinking at first that the disturbance was a pro-sovereignty demonstration, police called on leaders of the Hawaiian community for assistance.

"Everyone said they didn't know nothing about it," said Silva. "But they all wanted to go talk with her. At first we let some of them in [Liberty House], but they never come back out. Now we get plenty people, all kinds,

---

* It's Macy's now. Too bad. "Liberty House" was such a lovely name to use in this particular farce. And the mall itself was pointlessly rebranded as "Queen Ka'ahumanu Center." I'm telling you, in the old days people really knew how to name things.

wanting to go in there and join her, but we not letting anybody in."

All communication with "Ka'ahumanu" has taken place through her translator, a teenage girl from Paukukalo named Deeanne Pejoria. Pejoria was reported as missing when she vanished from Hana Bay on Saturday night. Dressed now in traditional Hawaiian kapa cloth, she no longer responds to her name and speaks only for the woman claiming to be the chiefess of old Hawai'i who died in 1832.

At one point during the police siege, Pejoria stepped out from Liberty House to deliver a message from Ka'ahumanu to the people of Hawai'i.

"I am in the House of Liberty. Why am I not free? And where are my free people? Why do they not come to me? I ended one kapu system. The time has come to end another one."

Continuing to speak for the alleged queen, Pejoria added, "Before, we needed to learn from the haole. Our people were dying. I thought it was our only hope, to get as much of their mana as possible. But where are my people today? Who has survived? Who among you is maka'ainana, a true child of the land? Ka'ahumanu asks this question."

Witnesses reported hearing only one comment in English from "Ka'ahumanu" herself, an observation that broke from her lips when she first saw the bronze statue dedicated to the shopping center's namesake.

She asked, "Who that fat old tutu?"

Third one. Same day, page five.

Identity of Missing Policeman Revealed

The Maui Police Department today released the identity of the officer missing since Saturday night. Detective Hector Ito of Pukalani vanished at Hana Bay while investigating mysterious lights flashing near the birth-cave of Queen Ka'ahumanu.

One police search party continues to comb the greater Hana area....

Fourth one. Wednesday's paper.

Ka'ahumanu Impostor Lashes Out at Costco Site
Mob of Followers Grows Steadily.

Accompanied by an ever-increasing swarm of followers, the Hawaiian woman who claims to be the returned spirit of Queen Ka'ahumanu left her hideaway in the Liberty House store at Ka'ahumanu Shopping Center. She led a noisy and destructive attack on the construction site for Maui's newest high-volume discount store, Costco.*

Her principal weapon is a fourteen-foot cannon, with which she blew enormous holes in the three-hundred-foot long cement-block wall intended to hold up the south end of the new store. One antique specialist who saw the cannon close-up claims it to be at least two hundred years old, of a type very commonly found on British frigates and warships.

Instead of cannon balls, the ragtag army fired pieces of the bronze statue of Ka'ahumanu that had recently been installed in the central courtyard of Ka'ahumanu Center. Witnesses say

★ At the time I first published this spoof, the walls of Maui's first Costco were beginning to rise. In 1870 the US Army built Fort Apache at the confluence of the north and east forks of the White River in Arizona. After the Battle of Hastings in 1066, the Normans started building castles all over England. The US has constructed seven hundred and thirty-seven military bases in foreign countries and has stocked them with two and a half million paid personnel. Do I detect a pattern here, or have I just been eating too much poi?

These days when Maui visitors arrive at Kahului International Airport and rent a car to drive to their hotel rooms, they first run a gauntlet of ultra-familiar consumption castles—Costco, Krispy Kreme, Kmart, McDonalds and Burger King, Lowes, Office Max, Sports Authority, Walmart, Home Depot, and a sheet-metal cathedral that residents sometimes refer to as "Godmart." All this, and the sky is pretty. No wonder people keep voting to elect Maui as the "best island in the world."

that the queen's head was the first body part to be used as artillery. When it pierced the enormous Costco wall, a cry rose from the mob of followers, who then used bulldozers and hand tools to create chaos at the job site.

Police stood by helplessly, having been ordered by both the mayor and by Governor Cayetano not to respond except to defend innocent lives.

"Until we know more about what we're dealing with here," said a spokesperson for Cayetano, "we'll be proceeding with a lot of serious reservations."

The self-proclaimed queen ended her thirty-minute attack by walking with her estimated two hundred or more followers up ʻIao Valley into the West Maui mountains. They have called for all the "real people" of Hawaiʻi to join them in a movement to "overthrow the haole kapu system."

Fifth one. Thursday's paper.

Missing Policeman Found at Remote Kaupo Site

Detective Hector Ito of Pukalani, missing since his strange disappearance at Hana Bay on Saturday night, was found late Wednesday on a rocky beach in Kaupo. Mystified and confused, he could recall nothing about the four days of his absence.

"I don't know," he said. "I was walking around the corner at Kauiki Head. Then there was light. I don't know."

122

Detective Ito was found wearing nothing but the traditional-style Hawaiian loincloth or malo. His uniform, gun, and other personal possessions are still missing.

☾

Part II
the lies continue

Part II—the lies continue

First one. Friday's paper.

"Queen" Gathers a Royal Following
Hundreds Mass at 'Iao

They arrive with oversized coolers, chain saws, air mattresses, folding chairs, rice cookers, battery-run televisions. When they get to 'Iao, they're told to leave the modern contraptions behind.

"Bring food, hand tools, and one change of clothes," they are told. According to rumor, weapons are being accepted, too.

An estimated two thousand two hundred people have moved into makeshift campsites near 'Iao State Park, rallying around their queen—a woman who died one hundred sixty-three years ago and who returned to life, they believe, last Saturday night in Hana.

An unidentified woman who calls herself Ka'ahumanu has been the focus of numerous public demonstrations this week, including a two-day interruption of normal business at Ka'ahumanu Shopping Center and an outburst of vandalism at the Costco construction site.

Authorities are still unsure what to make of this unexpected development. "We don't exactly know what she wants," said MPD spokesperson Detective Hercules Silva. "We don't know if this is some kind of hula festival or what."

Deeanne Pejoria, the Maui teenager who continues to speak for "Ka'ahumanu," has repeatedly delivered the following message:

"The Queen apologizes to the people of Hawai'i for her mistake in accepting the customs and values of the haole. She asks all her loyal subjects to re-dedicate themselves to Hawai'i nei."

People of all ethnic backgrounds have left their homes to gather in the West Maui mountains....

Second one. Same paper.

Stand-In Queen Can Expect A Bill

Royalty has its price, and Ka'ahumanu will be asked to pay hers. It won't be cheap.

As police and county officials hesitate, unsure exactly how to respond to the supposed return of the kuhina nui of old Hawai'i, the management of Ka'ahumanu Shopping Center is preparing for action.

The directors of Maui's biggest mall met today with representatives from Maui Land & Pineapple Company, Alexander & Baldwin, and the Costco corporation. The business leaders assessed damages and agreed on a plan that would help them recover the revenues lost during recent disturbances.

"We are prepared to file a lawsuit against Ka'ahumanu, if it comes to that," said assistant comptroller for Ka'ahumanu Center Helga Nokidoki. "We're hoping that the queen will respond reasonably, however, to a fair demand for compensation."

Third one. Sunday paper.

Monster Demands Will Pay Off State Deficit
Queen Gets Bill For $350 M

Ka'ahumanu was happy to make amends. But that was before she glanced at the bottom line.

In a dramatic confrontation, the so-called queen of Hawai'i and hundreds of her followers met yesterday with representatives from Ka'ahumanu Center, Maui Land & Pineapple Company, A&B Commercial Properties, and the Costco corporation.

The queen offered a formal apology to the business leaders and promised to "ho'opono," to make amends for damages to the Costco wall. She was struck speechless, however, by the unexpected size of the sum being demanded.

The queen walked proudly in the front of her followers, many of whom have adopted traditional Hawaiian garb. At six feet tall and heavily tattooed on her legs, hand, and tongue, eyes flashing and wild hair moving in the gusty winds of 'Iao Valley, "Ka'ahumanu" made an imposing, regal figure. She and her close advisors were dressed in kapa cloth stamped with intricate designs and draped with garlands of maile, ti, and other greenery.

The royal procession met head-to-head with its opposite, a long line of bureaucrats dressed in conservative business attire, most of them carrying laptop computers, briefcases, ledgers, and file folders stuffed with accounting sheets. Leading this entourage was assistant comptroller for Ka'ahumanu Center Helga Nokidoki, a thin, gray-haired bookkeeper from Indiana who moved to Maui only five years ago.

Nokidoki listened to Ka'ahumanu's offer to make amends, smiled slightly, then announced the payment due as three hundred fifty million dollars.

Explaining the large sum, Nokidoki named the damage to the concrete wall, destruction of a "timeless monument of public art," loss of income for the entire shopping center over a two-day period, and irreparable damage to the mall's public image.

"No one wants to shop at Ka'ahumanu Center if they think

someone like Ka'ahumanu could show up at any time," said Nokidoki.

When asked how these figures were derived, Nokidoki said, "We follow certain formulas. It's difficult to explain."

In an unexpected twist Nokidoki and her team announced that they would donate the queen's payment directly to the State of Hawai'i in order to compensate for the State's recently announced shortfall of three hundred fifty million dollars.

Several of the Queen's followers expressed astonishment that Ka'ahumanu's debt exactly equals the State's shortfall. When asked her opinion, Nokidoki repeated her earlier comment, "We follow certain formulas. It's difficult to explain."

Divided equally among Ka'ahumanu's estimated two thousand followers, the bill comes to one hundred seventy-five thousand dollars per person.

Fourth one. Monday paper.

Queen's Followers Vow To Work Off Debt

"The life of the land is preserved in righteousness."

These words translate the Hawai'i State motto, once coined by King Kamehameha III: "ua mau ke ea o ka 'aina i ka pono." Quoting this phrase, the alleged Queen Ka'ahumanu and her roughly two thousand followers announced today that they would work "no matter what it takes" to pay off their collective debt of three hundred fifty million dollars.

The county responded immediately by arranging positions in a wide range of programs for public benefit, including security guard work, roadside clean-up crews, yard maintenance teams for resorts and condominiums, janitors in public facilities and parking supervisors at the Kahului Airport.

Queen Ka'ahumanu herself will serve as the custodian at

Kamehameha III School in Lahaina.

Conservative estimates show that the debt will be fully paid in as few as eleven and a half years.

"Above all," said a spokesperson for Ka'ahumanu, "the people of Hawai'i must ho'opono. They must do what is right."

Fifth one. Almost exactly one year later.

Ka'ahumanu Spotted at Homeless Shelter

The woman popularly believed to be the resurrected spirit of Queen Ka'ahumanu was spotted standing in line for a hot meal at the homeless shelter yesterday.

"I know it was her," said Deeanne Pejoria, a Paukukalo teenager who volunteers once a week at the shelter. "I see that tongue with all the tattoos. So trippy!"

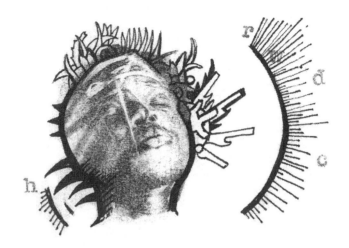

Several good reasons
NOT to be here now

Several good reasons
NOT to be here now

Take a deep breath. Now hold it.

What are the chances that you just breathed somebody else's air?

Let me be specific. You just sucked in a bucketful of air. Officially these molecules are now part of you. What are the chances that one molecule of this lungful was once a part of Julius Caesar's dying breath—the official last gasp of the founding henchman of the great Roman Empire as he was shishkebobbed simultaneously by dozens of his own political cronies? Do you think it's even possible?

Could you and Julius be so intimate as to share the same molecule? Imagine. For a while the molecule hung out in his earlobe, and then he exhaled it, and now it's circulating around in your kidneys, and tomorrow it'll be in somebody's bananas—like that? What are the chances?

Ninety-nine in a hundred.

That's what they say.* In fact, the odds are extremely good that you just sucked in a tad of old Julius right this moment.

Okay. You can let it out.

Two things happened to me today. I saw in the paper that Bumpy Kanahele, the Hawaiian sovereignty leader, has been arrested without bail for refusing to respect the civic authority that captured his people's kingdom about one hundred twenty years ago. He could be sentenced to five years in prison. They're refusing bail because Bumpy used angry, threatening language and frightened the representatives of

---

* *Innumeracy: Mathematical Illiteracy and Its Consequences,* by John Allen Paulos (Farrar Straus Giroux, NYC).

135

the civic authority.

Now for the second thing that happened, and it happened right after: I suddenly remembered this weird fact about breathing and Julius Caesar and the rest of it.

I even remembered where I'd read it, so (with some difficulty) I looked it up it again—in *What Counts*, a wonderful paperback collection of all the mind-jolting facts and statistics that *Harper's* magazine publishes each issue in its "Harper's Index" column. I remembered right.

With every breath, you breathe in a million pasts.

And directly above this strange fact, *What Counts* lists an even more curious statistic. It tells us how long "now" lasts.

Think about it. The present moment. It does exist, at least in our minds. If it exists, it must exist for a certain length of time. How long?

Here's another way to ask the question: if you think, "Oh, I'm really happy right now," how much time do you give yourself before you can start to feel insecure again? Or, when your boss (whoever he or she may be) says, "Do it now!"—how much time have you got before you begin to look deliberately unwilling?

"Harper's Index" says, "Estimated number of seconds that humans perceive 'the present' to last: 3."

One. Two. Three. Yep, that sounds about right to me.

The grand slogan of my generation was always "Be Here Now." I still hear people say it. I think I heard Bill Clinton say it the first time somebody shouted out, "Hey, what about that Whitewater investment?"

America is a very "now" culture, and Hawai'i never has been. Therein lies the dynamic of our lives.

Three seconds. Be here now, and that's all you get.

Suppose you actually could achieve the state of total be-here-now-itude. If you did live totally "for the moment"—and if you didn't weenie out—I think you'd want to drive your car as fast as you could off a sheer cliff on the road to Hana. You'd be willing to blow yourself up, and the whole world around you, just because you'd disrespect the past and future so vehemently.

I can't "be here now," and this is where I separate from my many wonderful spiritually minded friends. Many of them keep clutching and shaking their "now" like a big, noisy Christmas present. They believe that they truly aren't... whatever it is that they *think* they aren't. Some even believe that they aren't really named whatever they *thought* they were named.

But I could never change my name. To me, anymore, the past is just too fundamental.

My breath, my face, my thoughts, my community have all been delivered to me out of the huge past, and I can only reshuffle the ingredients to whatever extent that I can work my puny will power. I am all that I am made of, and all that I am made of has been shared around the planet with everything.

We're all just walking puffs of Caesar's breath. We're all a bunch of mad gardeners trying to keep up with the pruning. I don't believe that we create the plants and the soil.

My garden has real trees, not crystal nectar fountains. When I walk across the lawn, that's real dog poop I try to dodge. I don't mind acknowledging the past. The past is awesome and full of mystery.

I once had the chance to walk into the heart of a Neolithic temple over five thousand years old. Newgrange it's called. In Ireland. A "passage grave." Essentially, it's a man-made hill twice the height of a two-story house and as wide as a football field, created by Stone-Age people who cleverly stacked up an incredible number of unliftable boulders. These unknown builders decorated their special hill with a skin of bright white quartz stones, and they carved beautiful spiral designs into the raw rocks.

But that's just the beginning. When they built the hill, these skillful "cave men" left a passageway into the center so that they could stoop and crawl their way along a sixty-five-foot tunnel into a secret chamber at the very heart of their hill. This chamber is twenty feet high and big enough for a dozen people to stand upright. The builders also left three very short passages that spur out from the central chamber—three chapels, so to speak, almost like windows in a museum display. In each of these chapels they placed a hand-ground, bowl-shaped rock containing human ashes and cremated bones.

Try to imagine the reasons those people felt such intense devotion. To whom? To some Julius Caesars of their own time.

But Newgrange is much more than a Flintstone mausoleum. It's also a cosmic clock. Over the entrance, where you have to squat and use your hands to squeeze yourself into the passage, the stone that scrapes your back is a very carefully chosen, long, brick-shaped piece. And above it the builders left a slit, a horizontal keyhole.

When the sun rises on the morning of the winter solstice, the very moment when days start to lengthen and winter begins to withdraw, that heroic first sunlight of the new year runs right through the keyhole, pours straight down the passage, and lights up the central chamber like a pine-pitch torch.

Science meets poetry meets history meets religion.

These people had very sophisticated methods for measuring, calibrating, and constructing. Not many of us slick, modern types could make something like Newgrange no matter how many boulder-rolling brutes we had to help us.

Basically I think we're afraid of the past. The human race, exactly as it is today, has been around at least one hundred and fifty thousand years, and all that forgotten experience haunts us from our bones.

So we draw a veil over the past and imagine that pre-history was populated by dirty dimwits who went around questing for fire. None of them could tell a joke or sing a song. We also draw a veil over living cultures that remind us of our monstrous past. In fact we surround ourselves with these veils and hide. Just being here. Now.

That's a little like escaping from a mugger by slipping a number-fifty-six shopping bag over your head.

The problem is this—just because something's past doesn't mean it's gone. We inherit the past just as surely as we inherit our elbows and our teeth and our noses. And if you don't take care of your teeth, you're an idiot.

Bumpy knows that.

During that same summer that I crawled into the Newgrange passage grave, I had an even more intimate experience of just how nonessential the "now" is.

I was with an old Irishman, and we were traipsing around on the slopes of Carrowmore, a wind-swept grassy hilltop near Sligo. We were in he heart of the land of the fairies. Across the valley we could see the supernatural dome of a little mountain called Knocknorea. They say that once a year on a full-moon night a hidden door opens in the bottom of that hill, and out comes a precession of fabulous spiritual creatures led by the astonishing Maeve herself, the Faerie Queene. This parade of living memories then crosses the valley floor and disappears under a flat-topped mountain called Ben Bulben. The poet WB Yeats is buried near there, at his own request.

Well, this was late summer, the dry part of the year, but Irish rain —just as in Ha'iku—respects no season. Suddenly, the sky began to pelter us. We needed a shelter. The old guy said, "We can duck in here."

And what was it? Another passage grave, a somewhat shabby little thing, but big enough for us to huddle in there like two Cub Scouts in a pup tent.

I knew that cold rain was falling outside on the thick, thick wall of the little hill that sheltered me—though in the central chamber life was snug and dry. In the quiet of that Stone Age tomb we could hear each other breathing, each of us sucking in more of Julius Caesar's air.

No doubt the faeries and ghosts were moving about in the rain, perhaps even the ghosts of those sophisticated Stone-Age craftsmen who had assembled my haunted shelter.

My sense of my position in time began to slip, and slip cheerfully away. If it hadn't been for a few modern tokens—the ballpoint pen in my pocket, my belt-buckle—I might have come totally unglued and walked out of that passage grave into any century, any past you can imagine.

Bumpy, if I were sitting in that little passage grave again today, the first person I would think of would be you.

THE PRESENT

Even the green grass
is a stranger here, buddy

Even the green grass
is a stranger here, buddy

You are the person I admire, because you are a member of my tribe.

I stumbled after this thought—grabbed at it as a way to pull myself out of a terrible jam—last night while I was sitting outside. I don't know if you do this, but when I'm alone at night, I like to think. I try to remember how I think, after the phones shut up and the obligations pull back into the darkness to doze, until the early dawn gets them roused and howling and hungry again.

I dodge them by sleeping less.

But thinking can get you into trouble, and I admit it. Thinking can make you stutter, lose your wallet, change your name to something that no one wants to call you, stop eating what you like to eat, and forgive the unforgivable.

I was thinking about the grass around my house, and that's what got me started.

The grass around my house—and there's a lot of it, whatever tolerates the regular mowing and settles into something like what people from Los Angeles call a lawn—all of it came originally from seed that was brought to Maui in cattle feed on wooden boats that crossed the Pacific. And not very long ago.

I moved to Ha'iku for the sheer pleasure of blinding myself with the color and health of its green grass. I still remember my first sight of it, when I was driving a truck full of Lahainaluna students up Kokomo Road, though I can't quite remember when that was.

I feel that same rush of gladness every time I drive past Haku Baldwin's horse paradise with its sky-blue stables on the mauka side of Makawao Avenue,* that same eagerness to give up half of my dreams just to be around that quiet groundfire of breathing green.

The first horses came to Hawai'i on the sailing ship *Lelia Byrd* in 1803, the same year that foreign diseases came and started slaughtering Hawaiians in every village and every household. The very idea of ranching didn't arise here until the mid-1800s, and I really don't know when in that century my "lawn" arrived. Maybe one of you can help me with this.

I heard from a friend that the tall stand of pines crowning Giggle Hill**—fat-trunked and pole-straight and nearly limbless, crowded in rows like corn—were planted by pirates as insurance in case they ever got dismasted. I still have a hard time imagining the work involved in covertly dragging a new green mast down the footpaths from Kokomo to the shore, maybe Pauwela Point, maybe Makiko Bay.

I've read that Kauiki Head, next to Hana Bay, never had ironwoods, no trees, in the not-too-distant old days. I've heard that kiawe was introduced to force us to wear shoes. I understand that the deliberate introduction of the mosquito is a well-documented case. I'm a grown-up now; I no longer think that any of this was a very long time ago.

All these thoughts felt important because the night air barely moved. Power was rising out of the soil.

Distressed with thinking about the acres of that upstart malihini grass, I looked at other plants. The bananas were ready for anything, free now from the beating of the wind, too happy to actually care that they really belong in Malaysia or New Guinea. That they have no permission to be here.

All around me, the red ti plants were reaching for the most nearly unbearable union possible, their leaves bent in every possible attitude of yes. Their

*   Haku is gone now, but her horse paradise persists.

**   See the footnote about Giggle Hill in chapter two, page 16.

ancestors were brought here by Polynesians—or perhaps, since they are red and ornamental, by some early twentieth-century housewife-horticulturist whose ancestors had come here from Massachusetts. I found them at the dump. They are cuttings of cuttings of cuttings going way back. They are the very same plants that came here centuries go. And nothing was going to stop them from enjoying this windless night.

I was sitting on the lanai, the floodlight spilling on my lap. I'd built the cottage myself three years previous with materials shipped to me from a home supply outlet on the northwest coast of North America—sticks and plywood from mills in the Rockies, stain from a factory in Bellevue Washington, nails from a foundry in Strongsville Ohio.

Most of my news was coming from the cities of America. My shirt had been buttoned for the first time in Indonesia, and the Chinese had a hand in my trousers. The light that was falling on my lap burned down from hot, Mexican-made tubes fired by electricity from turbines that turn with burning black slick from Alaska. The truck I drive was shipped here on a barge.

We all like so much of what comes from distant places.

My golden retriever Makapuʻu was almost completely manufactured, through breeding, by European people now long dead who placed a great premium on fetching something—I don't know what. Knowing my dog, I'd also guess that these people put another great premium on totally agreeable personalities. Makapuʻu has almost no deeper wolf-nature, except when raw meat is involved.

He and I sat near each other on land that I "own" according to the teachings of my tribe. Because I work hard and pay money, a bank and the local government agree that this is "mine." Having this land gives me freedom and loneliness, as my new front gate indicates. My land could accommodate a very small village, but such a village is forbidden by the rules of this tribe. By law I must be alone here, within my own boundaries.

Most of the rules of my tribe were brought here from the

cities of the eastern shore of North America, before that from Britain—the notion that I should "own" some land, for example, and the concept that I can "own" but not "ranch and eat" my dog. I try to stick by the rules though I break a few every day.

Last night sitting in the dark I believed that it is the land itself, not us, who tries these things out. It's Haleakala, this mountain, that tries out a new coat of grass, a new group of people, a new set of tribal rules. The land is doing an awful lot of experimenting right now, and I try not to take these experiments too personally, nor too seriously.

But the tribe itself is personal. You, like me, are personal. We're all essentially homeless people enthralled with the home we use. We're all lucky to be here, and we know it, and I believe that each of us deep down somewhat begrudges the fact that nearly everyone else is here too.

Last week I attended a session of the Maui County Planning Commission. The question came up: What is a Hana resident? One of the commissioners suggested the idea that Hana stopped being "Hana" when the mill closed down in 1944. The only true Hana residents are those people who were living in Hana more than fifty years ago.

Such an idea makes planning very difficult, given the dizzy pace of experimentation that this land has been enjoying during the past, brief two hundred years.

None of us is sure—even though we dearly want to be—what the next move should be, or even if we have one. We're just starting to get ourselves organized here, and we don't even know what it is we've started.

In the silence last night, I could hear the soft roar of cars every so often getting close and going away. I always hope that they make the curve.

That driver is always someone I admire. Another member of our constantly possible tribe.

Don't worry about tsunamis,
watch out for moonlight

Don't worry about tsunamis, watch out for moonlight

The big moon of October is bearing down on us like a full-armed barmaid from Bavaria hoisting five brimming mugs in each hand high over the heads of the yelping and hollering crowd.

Where I live, the cows are yelling and bugling late into the night. I can't keep the lawn cut. Here at the sagging rear end of summer the plants are exhaling more than they're inhaling. The new leaves just can't belch fast enough.

My driveway is coated with smashed, fermenting guava fruits. Papayas, too. Yellow and orange fruit is rotting where it falls. The night air smells of jelly and dust. Large guava limbs have ripped away under the strain of their own weight and come crashing down. Banana stalks are toppling from the heaviness of their own sharp-ribbed fruit.

Along the roadsides, you see people fighting back against the heaving burden of leaves and branches. This is the month of mowers and Round-up and machetes, of road crews scraping the edges of the asphalt and gluing down new safety dots. Deep in the distant purple air the general quiet is hemmed by the faraway whining of chain saws.

Lots of mosquitoes. The stagnant ponds are thickening and swelling. We'll have mosquitoes till the first big gully-flushing rain builds up.

A fullness fills everything we do.

For the time being, we're just not worrying as much as. We have more than enough of. We've had our fill.

The whole atmosphere feels pumped up, as if we could see the long end of an enormous basketball-inflating needle sticking through the outside hull of the sky. Cats nearly every-where have, or want to have, children.

This is the month of ripeness and forgetting.

The trade winds have died so often over the past couple of months that we're in danger of forgetting the future. Clapping mosquitoes to death is not exactly the way we want to be remembered anyway.

Nothing can hurt us anyway. Last week the whole island survived a terrible tsunami which turned out to be nothing but a society-stopping ripple, a hoax, an unplanned freak holiday in a month of freakish and dubious holidays—Halloween, Columbus Day.

According to the Hawaiian historian David Malo, we're in the last month of the season of Kau, the vegetable maximum before the sun begins its slow decline to the south. Scorpio is sprawling above the horizon, its flat head pointing directly at the setting moon. If we hadn't set fire to all our bridges that connect us with the Hawaiian past, Malo says, our Makahiki season would be starting now. Sometime soon (in the old way) we would be paying our taxes.

We would be caught up in a public display of giving away our treasures. We'd be handing over swine and feathers, new bark cloth and bundles of surplus poi wrapped between planks of smoke-dried shark meat.

This is the month when all of us have to unload our excess so that we don't choke on it.

After all, Halloween is not really about spooks. It's about excess. The earth and its people have piled up a superabun-dance. Originally it was not children who went door to door. The poor and the needy were the ones who would mask them-selves then pound on the houses of the abundant, yelling "Give it away! Come on! Unload!" Halloween began as an old Irish festival of forced taxation: Disgorge, before you drown in all that! No one gets to sit and sicken on his hoard, not in the ooz-ing overflow month of October.

For this is the dangerous month of satisfaction. To "satisfy" is to make someone sad. I'm not making that up. I'm only reporting on the history of the word.

Watch out for satisfaction. The next step is coma.

In 1783 the first human being ever to leave the earth ascended eighty feet in the air for a five-minute hot-air balloon flight over Paris, France. Fourteen years later, another Frenchman stepped out of a hot air balloon that was more than two thousand feet in the air. He was hanging onto a twenty-three-foot diameter umbrella, thereby making the first parachute jump. Airplane inventor Wilbur Wright called this the most courageous act in aviation history.

The fact that this aerial pioneer succeeded only in pile-driving himself into a heap of *humain tartare* (or, as we say, sashimi) makes me question the precise use of the term "courageous." But I know why he jumped. I noticed the date.

Both of those stunts took place in the month of October, which makes total sense to me. October is the month to do the unreasonable and the impossible. Either that or go crazy while you clutch your stash.

So have a garage sale. Donate. Walk up to strangers and give them things. Confess. Empty the refrigerator. Spay the cat. Get to the dump. Shave. Cut your nails. Walk up and down the roads singing at the top of your lungs.

You want to unload.

Otherwise, that fat-ass harvest moon's gonna come hauling itself up over Mauna Kea, then over the shoulders of Haleakala, then come pouring down on you. And then you'll be too loaded-down to leap up out of its way. You might get trapped and smothered under an avalanche of moonlight, pinned there, conked out.

Then it'll take the thickest downpours of December to flush you free of that dream.

☾

He who has heart has heard
the harmonious ha-cha-cha

He who has heart has heard
the harmonious ha-cha-cha

Everyone whose last name starts with an "H," please stand up. Now the rest of you—applaud. Come on. No, no booing from the "B"s. No hissing from the "S"s. There we go. Okay. "H"s, you can sit down now.

Let's get on with it.

About a year ago I bought my first Rolodex,* which I took as a sure sign that I had become a grown-up. Prior to that I used to keep everyone's addresses and phone numbers neatly organized by writing them on scraps of paper and stuffing them into the back pockets of my jeans. That way if I needed to call someone all I had to do was rummage through the closet.

Sometimes, if a month or two had elapsed since my last call, I'd have to go to my back-up files. The laundry basket. And if I couldn't find them there—well forget it. They'd probably moved already anyway.

This organic filing system always worked well enough for me until the day I found one of my address scraps in the lint trap of the dryer. The dryer had hot-blown the paper without mercy until its tissue had transformed into something bony, like petrified dinosaur skin bristling with flakes and fuzz. It cracked apart as I unfolded it, and there in the blue blobs that had once been vital information I read the horrible news.

I'd lost my mother. Lost her phone number anyway.

So I went out and bought a Rolodex—

* Okay, I admit it. Fifteen years later, and now it sounds so ridiculous, so analog, to say that I bought a Rolodex. It's like bragging about your new blunderbuss or telling someone that you're looking for a phone booth. Nevertheless, I'm still using my Rolodex.

which (if you don't know) is a plastic caddy with clip-in cards arranged by dividers from "A" to "Z." When you buy the thing, it comes pre-arranged for you with all twenty-six letters of the alphabet and exactly fifteen blank cards for each letter. When you get a new address or phone number, you flip to the appropriate letter, pull out a blank card, write on it, then pop the card back into its alphabetized group.

The popular letters fill up first.

That's the problem, the problem with any alphabetized system. The "M"s fill up, and then you're sunk. You've reached your quota for "M"s, and from then on you start avoiding people named Matsumoto and Miller.

This condition can lead to anxiety and in some cases to actual fear of people named Matsumoto.

Instead of yielding to this anxiety I decided to attend a meeting of the local Rolodex Support Group. There I learned what to do when a popular letter fills up.

You go and steal a blank card from the "Q."

All year long I've been adding to my Rolodex, and all year long there's been a little race going on between the letters of the alphabet—a race to see whose section would be the first one to fill up and start duffing the "Q." And guess who won?

H.

Who could have guessed it? I've never thought of "H" as a popularity front-runner. In fact I've never thought much about "H" at all. But my Rolodex tells me that I know more people whose names start with "H" than any other letter.

"H?" What is it about "H?"

I pulled out the Maui phone book and started counting pages. "H," which spans eighteen pages, is the third most popular last-name initial in this community. It comes in just behind sneaky old "S" (twenty-one pages), and way behind number-one "M" (twenty-seven pages). I think "M" is a cheater because nine of its twenty-seven pages list organizations that start with the word "Maui." But hey, let's not quibble.

158

The point is, "H" is big on Maui. Same on Oʻahu. I counted white pages for that island too. "H" is the fourth most popular letter on Oʻahu.

Does this matter? I wasn't sure until I started to think about "H" and what it is.

Make an "H" sound. Go ahead. Flap your mouth open and drop your throat until you've opened a tunnel between your innermost you and the outermost everything. Tip your head back so God can look down the tunnel and see the pit of your belly button. Now flinch your solar plexus muscles. Air gushes out. Your air.

Your breath.

The only sound an "H" makes is the whispery friction of air hitting air. It's the only speech sound we make without rumbling our throats and twisting or touching our lips, tongue, teeth, palate or vocal cords. "Hhh" is nothing but air. The giving of breath.

The other sounds all have some trick to them. "Mmm" can be sexy, hungry, or gruff. "Sss" can let the air out your tires, or it can scare a cat. But "Hhh" is the most honest sound possible.

It is harmonious and haunting. It heats up the heart till you holler out to your ha-cha-cha boyfriend, "Hey! Ha-zit?"

Ha-llooooo!

Of course "Hhh" is involved in all our greetings, our aloha, when we thrust our private breath at those we love, from the lowliest "Ha-do?" to the highest "Hallelujah."

We do this because "Hhh" is the expression of "Ha," the Hawaiian outburst meaning life, the breath of life. If we are "ha" we are "in sync with life." If we're not in sync with life, we are "ha-ole." No ha. No alo-ha.

I am no expert in Hawaiian language though I have asked the guidance of those who are. So I speak now about ha "me ka haʻa haʻa." Humbly.

I am, and probably will always be, somewhat haole with my Hawaiian. All of us are haole about something, and each of us has a haole within. Out of touch with the breath of it. The spirit of it.

The ha.

In some way, all of us are haole except God Himself, who provides the ha that blows us all forward. Remember the opening scene in the Bible: "And the earth was without form, and void; and darkness was upon the face of the deep. And the Spirit of God moved upon the face of the waters."

This Spirit is the breath of God blowing the waters, stirring them up. The Hebrews called this breath of God "Ruah." Emphasis on the "ahhh."

And God puffed his Ruah into us, says the story: "the Lord God formed man of the dust of the ground, and breathed into his nostrils the breath of life, and man became a living spirit."

In fact the word "spirit" comes from the Latin word meaning "breath," and when we are "inspired," the divine breath is pouring into us, renewing our puny supply. When we yearn to reach the divine, we "aspire"—or breathe towards—and follow our "aspirations" toward perfection.

When we use up our puny supply of Hhh altogether, we "expire." Our spirit goes "ex." Out. To blow in the big wind.

Suddenly I remember a strange old book on my shelf called *Science of Breath*—published in 1904 by Yogi Ramacharaka of The Yogi Publication Society (Chicago). In the first chapter it says, "Life is but a series of breaths."

The book provides breathing exercises so that you can get your own ha lined up with the big Ruah. Using rhythmic breathing, says Mr. Ramacharaka, many yogis reached "the highest degree of spiritual attainment possible to man in this stage of his existence."

In other words the Hindus, the Jews, and the Christians all agree with the Hawaiians that "Hhh" is our direct link to God. And keep in mind that "Hhh" comes from the pit of the stomach, not from the top of the brain.

Our souls are a kind of mist, rising. This fact was proven on the ancient battlefields, where in the aftermath of slaughter a visible mist would hover above the slain. Physically this mist was caused by the outgushing of so many overheated body fluids spewing from all the beheaded corpses. For the poet, though, as he gazed across that quiet landscape of hacked meat, the souls of the dead were rising to heaven in eerie plumes of steam.

The final ha.

In order to see this soul-steam whenever they wanted, the American Indians lit up their sacred pipes. So says Black Elk, the Oglala Sioux visionary who survived "Custer's Last Stand" and the massacre at Wounded Knee to tell his own story. *Black Elk Speaks* begins with the old warrior packing red willow bark into his pipe and lighting up. By-the-by he tells how the Sioux first got the idea of smoking, and the story goes like this:

Two warriors are out scouting on a far distant hilltop when suddenly they see, coming toward them from the mists in the north, a beautiful young woman dressed in fine white buck-skin. One warrior, the foolish one, gets into singles-bar mode and starts making some moves on this pretty lady. She says, "Oh yeah? Come on and try it."

A white mist covers the warrior and, when it passes, he's lying on the ground, nothing but rotting, maggot-covered bones.

The beautiful goddess turns to the other warrior and says, "Get back to your village and tell them to build a ceremonial tepee for me. I'm coming for a visit."

So he does, and they do. And one day the goddess comes sailing in from the north carrying a pipe with eagle feathers hanging from it. She sings:

With visible breath I am walking.

"And as she sang," says Black Elk, "there came from her mouth a white cloud that was good to smell."

In other words, for Black Elk the puff of smoke is the divine breath made visible, a miracle in which the Ruah takes on physical form.

Seen in this light, anti-smoking fanatics seem to be the biggest ha-oles of them all. Could anything be more sacrilegious than the no-smoking section of a restaurant?

(In fairness I have to point out that Black Elk wasn't talking about Lucky Strikes three packs a day. If he was, the Surgeon-General would be right to remind us of another famous Oglala Sioux saying: "Today is a good day to die.")

After delivering this fanciful story of the killer mist and the smoking goddess, Black Elk says, "This they tell, and whether it happened so or not I do not know; but if you think about it, you can see that it is true."

The difference between whether something happened (which we can't be sure of) and whether it is true (which we can know by thinking from the pit of our stomachs)—it's all a matter of breath. If we are "ha," we can know it is true. If we are "haole," we can waste plenty of time arguing over whether or not it really happened.

I feel that way about every scripture, myth, fable, and poem. Each of us has to be alert for the haole within. And I say this "me ka ha'a ha'a."

I wanted to write this article to prove that Hawai'i is the homeland of ha, where the Ruah blows clear as in the old days and in the wisdom of all beliefs. My proof was in my Rolodex and the white pages of our phone books.

So for contrast I went to another phone book, from a place that you might consider the heartland of haoles—Orange County, California. But I failed to prove my theory.

There, "H" is the fifth most popular last-name sound.

And my own Rolodex refuses to let me voice a prejudice, for the "H" names there come from a harmony of two handfuls of homelands. Hunter (English), Hoffman (German), Hermes (Greek), Hamamura (Japanese), Hafoka (Samoan), Hennessey (Irish), Ho (Chinese), Hoopii (Hawaiian). When it comes to Ruah, there are no chosen people.

So I say with all my ha to those of you who bear the initial of divine breath into this polluted world—mahalo. Thank you. Keep doing your easy job, please. And if you look for me, I may be gone, gone to visit the most secret, least known bay on this haunted and harmonious island. I won't tell you where it is. Only its name.

Hahaha.

If you must have a personality,
then please show it off

If you must have a personality, then please show it off

For What's-his-name

The date's already set for Saturday, June 3. We're going to have an annual festival for Ha'iku, call it the Ha'iku Flower Festival. I'm not sure how the idea got started.

But I think it's a good one.

I am curious to see all the people of Ha'iku in one place—stepping shyly forth from their gulches and banana patches and ranch houses and shacks, blinking and staring around at all the funny-looking strangers.

I'm telling you. A lot of saints and a lot of sinners. A group with lots of personality!

I could tell you some stories—but I won't. Not in the public press. Besides, this ain't no dot-dot-dot column.

Well, I might tell one or two. Just to prove that Ha'iku has a lot of personality.

Because this festival has got to reflect the Ha'iku personality.

And what could that be? Well, it must be made up of all Ha'iku people's personalities combined fifty-fifty with the larger personality that we build semi-consciously through our collective interactions—how we drive on the road and how we shop, what kinds of businesses we own and to what degree our streets are safe. That sort of thing.

The big question is this: what's gonna happen at the first Ha'iku festival? What would suit the Ha'iku personality?

I imagine a titanic backhoe-wrestling contest. Then an earth-moving competition. Have a race to tear up the Pukalani bypass. Or dig tunnels under it.

Anything involving water—especially heavily moving water or water that falls in large sheets—would allow us to show off our acquired skills. A race pushing cars through chest-deep, gushing floodwaters. A sand-bagging contest.

Create a thirty-foot-wide raging torrent and send it across somebody's property. Give each team six shovels, and an 'o'o, four cases of Budweiser, a telephone....

No. Too complex.

Run a cable across Maliko Gulch and let people zip across with a pulley.

Of course, various demonstrations side by side would reveal the many contradictions in Ha'iku's personality. The animal butchering demonstration, for example, would draw the crowds that the blue-green-algae smoothie bar would never miss. We'd need an air-brushed pickup truck and tinted-windowed car show, of course, but I think we should also offer an I've-dropped-acid car show and set up a special booth for the "Dare For Drive Slow" Society with its bumper stickers and buttons.

Please address your suggestions for Ha'iku Festival events to Untested Ideas Editor, P.O. Box 1033, Haiku HI 96708. I need your ideas because I just can't keep my attention on the problem. My mind is totally occupied by another train of thought— I mean, what is "personality" anyway?

How did we get one? Where did it come from? Some people are born with more personality than others apparently. Why is that?

Most of all, is a personality contagious? And if you've got one, can you take herbs for it or something?

I was raised with the idea that my personality came with me when I was born and it's going to stick with me even after my body drops. Think so? After I'm dead, no matter what happens—whether I'm stuck getting my punishment or I'm jumping from this body to a new body—will my personality still be with me?

In the afterlife will I still dislike cats?

Lots of people say so, Christians and Hindus alike. To them, we are who we are, dead or alive, whether we live in Haʻiku or drift like a gas from planet to planet.

But the other way to look at it makes more sense to me. In the other view my personality is just one of my body parts, like my toenails or the way my hair smells. I lose it when I lose the whole package.

In this view my soul does go on after I die, but my soul is no more different from your soul than any one frosted sixty-watt light bulb is different from any other. Soul-wise, we're each just one more unit of the great cosmic goo.

The Elizabethans felt this way. They believed that the personality is a physical defect.

They believed that the personality is a problem you have with your body that you should correct by watching your diet and by taking herbs and things.

For them, the best people lack personality altogether.

The Elizabethans got this idea from the ancient Greeks, and they applied it to their practice of medicine. I'm speaking here about the people of England some three to four hundred years ago, Shakespeare's time, not very long ago at all—modern people who spoke exactly the way we do except with a kind of verve and a set of interests that we reserve for other purposes.

They also believed that gold is a shade of red.

That's how fragile our deeply held beliefs can be.

Imagine what this means. Your personality, the "real you" that your best friend knows all about—your edginess, your fears, your excitements, what makes you laugh, what gets you horny, what gets you fighting mad, what makes you gloomy and withdrawn—these are symptoms of your uniquely diseased and imbalanced state.

According to the old belief, we each have four different kinds of fluid moving around in us, liquids sloshing and mixing between our gizzards and our intestines. "Humors" they called them, as in the word "humid." Sloshing and oozing.

Each liquid drifts in a different direction. One makes us

excited, one angry, one stubborn, and one depressed. These four juices mark the four extreme corners of the human personality.

Our personality is a circus running around between these four reactions: 1) manic and hysterically eager (sanguine), 2) explosively furious (choleric), 3) downright refusing to participate (phlegmatic), 4) exquisitely self-absorbed (melancholic).

The goal of Elizabethans was to balance these fluids until the traits canceled each other out. If you've got all your fluids in perfect balance, none will stick out and make a fuss. You will live without any of the four extremes of personality. You will be good-humored.

I see good-humored people all the time—I think. Of course, I forget to notice because these good-humored people have no personality.

I remember that one guy, though—what's-his-name.

Oh, never mind.

Thank God for good-humored people. Thank God for the guy who changes his name to "I. Breathed Yeast" and speaks very softly from that day forth. For shoppers who always have the right amount of change. For good people who are baffled by the stories they read in the newspaper. These people keep the world safe and competent.

I hope we'll have a special area for them at the Haʻiku Flower Festival. A booth for "Personality-Free People." These are spiritual people. They represent the soul, the soul that we will all, one day, be nothing else but. The sixty-watt bulb.

If I see a sixty-watt bulb person running for political office, I always vote for her or him. I want only good-humored people in office writing bills that will restrict my freedom. I think I myself once hoped to become a sixty-watt bulb.

I can't seem to be friends with sixty-watt bulbs. All of my friends have personalities.

They all have these defects, where one humor dominates another, and they have these wild swings—from raging fury to laughing at the top of their lungs, and then to thinking about what it all means and how ridiculous it all is, and from there to sadness.

Or they move in a different sequence. But they do move.

The pulse of their swings and their long resistances make up the painful and dangerous dance they dance—the cha cha cha of flesh and blood.

The good-humored man, by contrast, slips painlessly through as if he's been waxed.

The good-humored woman refuses to get involved in emotional outbursts. In that stillness, she makes room for a higher intelligence that guides her and all those about her. She is a wet, jelly-thick lake of calmness and joy.

I don't think she lives in Ha'iku. I'm sure I've never met her. Or did I? Nah. Can't remember. What's her name.

But let's set up a booth for the good-humored anyway and see if we notice anybody showing up. The rest of us can snort and spit and belly-up to the bad-humored places with all the flashy fury and unexpected impulses that make me me, you you, and Ha'iku... well, guess who.

Because these odd humors are not eternal. Therefore, they are precious.

The other morning I was out on the streets, running. (I do that sometimes, to pay for my sins.) It was dawn. I came up to the top of a steep section of the street, a long grade that always makes my head spin and my blood panic. I was running straight into the just-risen sunlight. In front of me on the roadside I could see a butchered carcass.

The remains of a pig.

The bones were red where all the meat had been sliced away. The rib cage and keel stuck straight up into the morning sky, the thin, bacon-like tissue stretching like a veil across a striking architecture of ribs and backbones. Sunlight glowed through this thinly stretched flesh, which shone with a serenely rich, rose-colored light. Almost a gold.

This was a terrible lampshade of life's precious beauty. Something to read by.

I'm all for celebrating personality if only because it will be gone so soon.

☾

Nothing this strong and good can
truly pass from the world

Nothing this strong and good
can truly pass from the world

I'm a mongrel just like most of you—the result of a lot of un-planned and random breeding. My ancestors, God bless 'em, seemed to like variety.

And who can blame them? They were common people, not blue-bloods, not purists. The whole human race was fair game to them because they knew their place—right in the middle of it all, rubbing elbows with the whole furry human pack, no matter where they traveled.

I can understand why they didn't want to marry the girl or guy next door. What's the fun of smooching someone who looks, smells, and sounds just like you? Anybody can have that experience.

Just pull the covers over your head and start singing.

No. I think they liked the glamour of the thicker hair, the whiter skin, the browner eyes, the whatever-it-was that they themselves didn't have. They liked the eternal mystery of mar-riage to some foreigner, someone they would never ever really understand. They were probably life-long curious to find out what their crossbreed kids were going to look like.

Take my grandfather, for example.

He was a white man and he fell in love with a girl from an island race, from a people considered (until quite recently) savage, inferior, untameable.

He was of Yorkshire English stock, and he passed down that blunt name you see on the title to this book, the name that Hawai'i folks have such a hard time getting right—they always want to make it "Woods," I think because the real name seems to end too soon. I even have a jacket made in Hong Kong that has my name stitched inside: Paul Wooo.

He was a white man, I tell you, but he never sold rum to the natives, never broke a treaty, never swindled a brown man out of his land. He fought disease. He was a doctor. He had no office. He walked to his patients' houses, and he opened up the family parlor at night for the laboring people. When he died and his casket sat in that same parlor, long lines formed in the street, people waiting patiently in the heat of the sun, waiting for a chance to say goodbye to Doctor Wood.

History drives me into a fury, the news of white people especially, the madness reported on television, but I have never apologized for my name.

Only a broken man would ever deny his grandfather, especially one such as this man.

But imagine the trouble this man caused his Methodist parents when he announced that he'd fallen in love with a dark-eyed, vivacious little savage girl. Worse yet, she wouldn't marry him unless he gave up his religion and took on hers—an ancient religion full of symbolism, mystical experiences, chanting, and the rituals of cannibalism.

If a man is religious about his religion (and apparently my granddad was), then he can't go switching on command. There's the whole business of conversion. He knew about Saint Paul on the road to Damascus. He knew that conversion strikes you suddenly and involuntarily, like a bolt of lightning. Or else it grows on you slowly, like warts. I think my granddad argued for the "let's get together and see what happens" approach.

She told him to come back when he'd converted. She'd give him six months.

He took five and a half.

And thus the tribal influence came to topple the Methodist, both in Doctor Wood's heart and in mine.

What kind of people were my grandmother's people?

They were islanders who had crossed the wild sea to settle a lush, green, snake-free paradise somewhere around 800 BC.

They never developed a civilization, never knew what that meant until civilization was forced upon them in the eighteenth century. They walked on paths, not streets. Their lives were organized around the extended family. They had no politics, no state, no central government. They never built a town.

They fought among themselves to secure or expand group-held territory. Occasionally a strong man would arise to dominate a large realm, even the whole island for a time. They fought recklessly, naked and screaming. Legends say that their warriors could make incredible leaps, could even jump up onto spears in flight, would fall into monstrous battle furies that have been described as "warp-spasms."

A special class of priest-poets, both men and women, kept alive the traditions, histories, and genealogies of this culture. These bards knew magic and practiced medicine. They moved freely from place to place, welcome wherever they traveled.

Most importantly my grandmother's people loved place. They lived free, casual lives under the open sky. Their songs are filled with a celebration of the rain, the beasts, lovemaking, the small details of human experience.

They believed that the gods themselves dwell on the Earth. If one of these people felt it was time to go to Heaven, then he or she would get into a boat and paddle across the open sea, because Heaven is on Earth just over the horizon.

They accepted Christianity without shedding a drop of blood (although a deadly plague that killed half of their people motivated their willingness to accept the European God). They resisted the advancement of English-speaking culture until they could resist no more. Eventually, their native tongue was banned from the schools of their own land. Today, although street signs preserve the old names and books preserve the grammar, few people speak that language in everyday conversation.

Today these people appear to be civilized. When I'm filling out a governmental form and I'm asked to check boxes to identify my ethnic background, I never see a box that describes my grandmother's people—in fact, my people. These people are assumed to have passed from the Earth or else transmogrified into "Caucasians," whatever those are.

My grandmother was a Celt.

She, like the majority of my ancestors, was Irish. And by the way that word "Celt" is pronounced with a hard "K" sound, not like that band of has-been basketball players from Boston with their "Seltic," a deliberate British mispronunciation that makes my blood boil and then I feel a warp-spasm coming on.

Most of all, don't ever call me a "haole."

My people have been insulted, shot, starved, driven into exile, beaten into submission, scattered across the planet. If you ever hear an Irishman say "the luck of the Irish," you'll know how deeply ironic, even sarcastic that phrase can be.

And yet I once had the pleasure of standing in front of a group of three hundred Maui people on St. Patrick's Day and asking everyone with even a drop of Irish blood to raise a hand. Two hundred and seventy-eight hands went up.

You see, the Irish are good for something.

So on March seventeenth you can be sure I'll be lifting a glass of whiskey to the old folks. Come join me, and then we can have a long talk about cultural oppression, about sovereignty, about the extinction of cultures.

An article in the paper recently was telling that human languages are dying off, becoming extinct just like so many plants and animals. Like it or not, we're living in a time when variety is being sacrificed for uniformity.

They say that twenty to fifty percent of the world's languages even now are no longer learned by the children. These languages are "the living dead." Of the world's six thousand languages, only six hundred are assured of survival a century from now.

The Celts have had the lead over so many other cultures and languages in this dying game. Or is it really a dying game?

Can anything this strong and good truly pass from the world? When I lift my glass on the seventeenth, I'm going to say no. I don't speak the Celtic tongue, live in a crannog, raise cattle, nor when I want to die will I row my way to Tir na Nog in a coracle.

But I have a Celtic hand, and through it rushes the blood of the Sullivans and the Kellys and the Devlins—mingled with other mongrel bloods, and the mix is a good mix. I'm better and stronger for the mix. I'm an alloy of toughness. I have the mind and mouth of a druid, made wiser by my ancestors' vaster experience.

You can say as much about yourself, in your own way, no doubt.

And when the wind stirs the thick grasses here where I live, and the sudden rains come blowing and clothing my house and this land and all those about me—why, I'm telling you, I look out at this place with eyes that are older than my own eyes.

I could swear I'm right back where I belong.

For thanks,
I give you a hole in the ground

For thanks,
I give you a hole in the ground

Tomorrow I'll clean out the imu pit. I'll make sure I still have enough unfractured rocks for another good firing.

Tomorrow is the day before Thanksgiving.

I'll finish cutting up the kiawe logs I brought in last weekend.

To get those logs, we took a two-day scramble around East Maui, and we didn't get back home till the first edge of dawn Monday. We were driving back on the Hana road in the cloud-lit, fading moonlight (or was it queerly early dawn?) with a can of warm Mountain Dew between us and Monk's "Ruby My Dear" turned down low.

It's imu time.

My cooking utensils include a chain saw and a contractor-size wheelbarrow.

I snapped a shovel handle the other day. Two Haʻiku winters is about all a shovel can take before the wooden handle turns to chalk. So, as odd as it sounds, I've got to buy a new shovel so I can cook the holiday turkey.

After all, I'm cooking a feast for a small tribe.

I'm going to cook a turkey and a leg of lamb, and I'm going to cook them in the style of this land and of its people. (If you're a vegetarian, you'll have to forgive me for talking so bluntly about meat.) If my small tribe were larger, I'd gladly put even MORE meat in my imu. I'd prefer to cook meat that I've raised or hunted myself, but that won't be the case this year. Instead, I pay Foodland to raise or hunt for me. Maybe next year I'll achieve the perfect relationship to my food.

Once again this year, I'm cooking thanksgiving in a fiery hole that shouts to the sky.

Once again this year, I'm going to make the Pilgrims of Plymouth Rock run aground in Polynesia. Once again, The Great White Figureheads will have to stop staring into the heavens and turn to look instead at a pit in the earth.

The Pilgrims' prayer from the pit: *Out of the depths I cry to You, O Lord. Let my prayer be acceptable in Thy sight.* May the fire rise true, may the wood burn all the way across, may the food cook thoroughly, may the tribe be fed. May the party be loud and remembered if at all with embarrassment.

That pit, its walls darkened and maybe even glazed with the heat of earlier firings, still holds the clean, black, many-pitted, remembering stones. Those stones—round, black, glistening wet, smoky smelling—have sat together waiting under a board in the dark. "Pohaku" is the proper name for them. For months they've mumbled together down there like forgotten gods, unvisited except by occasional large insects or spiders. They're ready to glow red-hot again in my purposeful volcano.

On the night before it all begins I will pull the pohaku out of the pit and set them out in the starlight. Some will have crumbled from heat exhaustion. New stones will join—pitted, rounded, a precious resource, lava ready for reheating.

Thursday at sunrise I'll stack the dry kiawe and flammables in the imu, building them up around an eight-foot rod that prods vertically out from the base of the pit. The rod will hold itself like a thumb stuck right into the core of the future fire.

Then I'll skin the carefully built wood stack with a thick crust made of those black stones. Then I'll yank the rod our from the pile center.

For a minute, that open shaft will swallow the power of the zenith straight down. Then the fire will go in.

A fat plume of harmless smoke will surge up into the turbulent Ha'iku sky. And then a great fire will be held in the pit there, contained by earth and stone. I always imagine the fire going straight into the heart of Pele's mountain.

After that, we wait for the stones to sink into the ashes of the spent kiawe. We gather palm leaves from the land around the imu pit, our dinner ware. Only thirty feet away banana stalks are beaten and broken open. When the moment is right, thicknesses of juicy stems are heaped, steaming, down in the pit over the red-hots.

Women bring forth green baskets of feasting, the food woven and swaddled in leaves. These are lowered like messages into the rising furnace. The top of the heap is then overheaped with more plants, then with narrowing screens of fabric, then the whole fervent oven is totally scarfed in dirt.

Now the feast is a complete secret.

We spend at least half an hour watching for smoke vents— leaks—which the small tribe takes turns attacking with spade- fuls of earthy smother. Even an hour or two later people are still saying that they see some smoke coming from the imu. These people are committed to the imu.

The imu is the center of a universe that makes sense to me, and for that I give my howl of happiness delivered without a trace of irony, no fooling.

The imu ties me to the world, it ties me in every direction. Its stones tie me to the heat of the earth, and as the smoke rises that same heat ties me to the tumbling heavens. My tribe con- verges on this single spot, knitting its intentions together through many small orchestrated chores. Then the pit is opened. The good food is passed from hand to hand.

Eating is never the important point of a feast like this. Eat- ing is humdrum and private and, in the end, nothing but crap. The doing is everything. The tying-together.

Let the food spill forth. Taste a little, then give it all away. Let no one go hungry! Let nothing go to waste! We are here to act out the rituals of connectedness: Human bound to Earth and to Sky and to Tribe, Human fully alive in the intricating Now....

And I'm forgetting the Past, too, and that's not right, for the imu ties me even tighter to the past than it does to the present.

I have many histories, but my most important history is the history of the land that feeds me, the land I care for. On Thursday dawn as I set fire to the stones and the earth, I will lift my heart in gratitude to the Hawaiians who have taught me how to live here. I have been a slow but willing student.

Before I began writing this article, I intended to celebrate my freedom—the fact that I can shut my gate on the world and spend whole days far from the choked streets of Kahului, the clutter of Kihei, the high-rise insults of Honolulu.

I intended to celebrate the fact that Kmart is way, way down there, that all supermarkets are inconveniently far away. So far, my life is still good, still as I would choose it.

But why should I be so profane, when this may be my last moment under this moist sky, tonight's rain my last wetting, this shovelful of earth my final purposeful act?

Stone, fire, stem, flesh. These are my sacraments. A spadeful of earth lifted into the heavens. The imu ties me and lashes me into place.

God's belly button. The piko of my life.

And I am happy to be here, at the center of everything.

GLOSSARY

Glossary

'A'a - Rough-style lava rock, common on Maui. Giant-cheese-grater type ground.

A&B - Alexander & Baldwin, Incorporated, the Maui firm (est. 1869) generally considered responsible for everything—for Hurricane Iniki, for World War II, for the tidal wave of 1946, for every car accident, extraterrestrial sighting, sunburn, and unspayed pet on this island for the past one hundred years. In addition to that, also responsible for pretty much owning Maui.

Ahi - the yellowfin tuna, a big fish often spotted hanging around in sushi bars.

Aloha - Kindest regards. Good vibes. The earnest desire to be a fine person.

Auwe! - Oh no!

Brah - Term of address suitable if one or more of the following conditions apply: 1) man is wearing rubber slippers; 2) man has pig carcass tied to hood of truck; 3) boy; 4) man is standing in front of marijuana field with shotgun.

Captain James Cook - William Shatner's role model. An industrious farmboy from Yorkshire England who became one of Western history's greatest maritime explorers. Hawai'i's first recorded tourist. He sailed past Maui's North Shore in 1778 so as not to miss his rendezvous with death in a Big Island brawl.

Chicken skin - Horripilation.

Choke - A large amount. (Question: "How much stuffs you get already?" Answer: "Choke! Only planny! Like try?"

Downhill bikers - Those who ride bicycles from Haleakala (10,031 feet elevation) to the sea, a thirty-five-mile trip which takes about ten minutes if you go for it on your own and all day if you pay plenty to get into an incompetent lineup with other tourists who, like you, are all wearing pink football helmets.

Gravity Resistant Sky-Popper - A perfect example of why your father was right when he warned you not to believe everything you read. For a complete set of design plans, send $500 to this address.

Haole - Whitey; honky; round-eyed imperialist devil; outsider; destroyer of all that is sacred. (See "A&B.")

Heiau - Rock platforms erected by the Hawaiians as sacred sites, temple compounds, and seats of authority.

Hippie - Any haole (q.v.) who is A) not employed by A&B or the County of Maui and B) not filthy rich.

Ho'opono - to correct; to behave correctly.

Imu - Traditional Hawaiian earth oven: hot-rock underground cooking with banana and ti leaves and stems, the results suitable for feeding tribes.

Ka'ahumanu - Hawaiian queen (1777–1832) who governed the islands for thirteen years, during which time she tossed out the entire system of native faith and government and imposed missionary-twisted, Western-style thinking. In doing so, she slowed the extinction of her own culture. She was an intelligent and forward-thinking leader, and for that reason she has become the namesake of Maui's largest shopping mall.

Kahoʻolawe - An island in the County of Maui formerly dedicated to the god Kanaloa, from ancient days the training grounds for the heroic science of Poynesian open-sea navigation. In the early 1940s the US military seized the island and began using it as a bomb-dropping practice site. For the next fifty years the US blasted the shit out of this small Hawaiian island. Isn't that weird? When Hawaiian citizens began to die in protest of this practice, the US military withdrew and left behind its litter of twelve thousand tons of scrap metal, six thousand unexploded bombs, and a devastated island whose single cause of rejoicing would have to be that no human beings would be able to romp over its slopes for at least a few millennia. You think I'm making that up but I'm not.

Kahuna - any respected Hawaiian authority with specialized training in a field vital to the survival of the culture. Any Hawaiian priest/doctor/craftsperson/balladeer/scientist/druid.

Kalo (taro) - *Colocasia esculenta*, a marsh plant with large fleshy leaves that stores nourishment in its corm or submerged lower stem. Polynesians carried it from the East Indies throughout their Pacific migrations. Only the Hawaiians created a culture founded on kalo, which they made possible through sound engineering practices and a dedication to social agreements.

Kamehameha - The Hawaiian strongman (1753–1819) who took advantage of post-Captain-Cook chaos to seize control of the entire island chain for the first time in its history. When he died everything fell apart. The first boatload of New England missionaries arrived one year later.

Kapa - or "tapa cloth," an aboriginal Hawaiian fabric made by laboriously pounding, layering, and softening certain kinds of bark and then stamping and dyeing designs.

Kapu - Forbidden. A formal announcement that something is off-limits or not-to-be-done. (Tahitian version of this word: taboo.) The rules that governed pre-contact Hawaiian life are called collectively "the kapu system." In the midst of the emotional agony that followed the 1891 death of Kamehameha (q.v.), the Hawaiians themselves rejected the entire kapu system in a single moment—a banquet at which women and men ate freely together. At the head of the table, so to speak, was the most decisive and most elusive figure in Hawaiian history, Keopuolani (q.v.).

Kauʻiki Head - A large puʻu (cinder cone hill) now overgrown with ironwood trees that is the dominating landmark on the right arm of Hana Bay.

Keopuolani - The sacred wife of Kamehameha and mother of his heirs. Out of respect for the kapu that swathed her in both life and death, I will say only this: her ancestors were divine, and she was divine. She alone had the authority to dash the entire belief system that maintained her divinity, which she did in 1819. Then she embraced Christianity and established Maui's first Christian encampment, Waiola Church in Lahaina. A cenotaph there today suggests that her bones still lie next to the church, but I doubt it.

Kiawe - A thorny hardwood tree introduced to Hawaiʻi in the 1840s. Mesquite. It grows wild in the lowlands. Best wood for firing the imu.

Lahainaluna - District on the uphill side of Lahaina Maui, home of the oldest school west of the Rockies. The old missionary printing house here cranked out bibles, textbooks, and paper money, each a nail in the coffin of traditional island culture.

Liberty House - This was our home-grown Macy's, the foundation tenant of Ka'ahumanu Shopping Center. Now it's Macy's.

Limu - Seaweed, especially if you eat it.

Local - The opposite of haole (q.v.), which is all extremely simple except when you run into a local who isn't very local or a haole who is. And yet the only way you can really be local is because one or more of your grandparents did contract labor for the big sugarcane or pineapple plantations.

Lo'i - A traditional kalo-growing patch that is constantly flooded and refreshed with mountain water.

Maile - A native Hawaiian forest vine with subtly pungent foliage. A maile lei is made by stripping strands of bark and leaves away from the plant's tough inner fibers then twining those aromatic strands together. The gift of such a lei is a sure sign that somebody thinks you are pretty darn great.

Maka'ainana - The common people; the tribe. One interpretation: "eyes of the land." David Malo in *Hawaiian Antiquities*: "The commoners were the most numerous class of people in the nation, and were known as ma-ka-aina-na; another name by which they were called was hu. (Hu, to swell, multiply, increase like yeast.)" Jesus in *Luke*: "Blest are you poor; the reign of God is yours."

Makai - See Mauka/makai.

Makani - Wind, breeze; gas in the stomach.

Makapiapia - Boogers in the eyes.

Malama - To care for, preserve.

MEO bus - Maui Economic Opportunity, Inc., a county-wide social service organization, has little buses that will pick you up and drop you off. The old folks are hip to this.

Missionary - uninvited know-it-all. "Moral indignation is jealousy with a halo." - HG Wells.

Moke - An unflattering group label for any tough local guy.

Musubi - a ball of rice that you can carry around until you feel like eating it. Generally served with a plank of fried Spam on top, the whole package wrapped in nori, edible black seaweed.

Niʻihau - A small, mysterious Hawaiian island inhabited only by Hawaiians. No one's ever been there, no one ever talks about it, and I'm sorry I even mentioned it.

ʻOha - After you harvest the kalo, you take the ʻoha—the living stem with the top of the root—and replant it. That's continuity. That's culture.

ʻOhana - All the ʻoha together: the family, the big family, the tribe.

ʻOkole - Rear end; derriere.

Opihi - Shoreline limpets, that is sea snails. A popular wild food, raw or grilled. Pop 'em off the rocks down where the waves are crashing.

ʻOʻo - Digging stick.

Pele - Every force needs a face. That's how we humans operate with our self-absorbed imaginations. Pele (Pay-lay)— explosive, contentious, ever-shifting, sometimes voluptuous,

Malihini - Stranger, newcomer, foreigner; guest. Handy and Pukui in *The Polynesian Family System in Ka'u, Hawai'i*: "...she was kama'aina, for she was the native "daughter of the land" (kama'aina) who took the strangers (malihini) to see places of interest."

Malo - The man's loincloth. Handy and Pukui: "In explaining near kinship a kupuna would say, Nou ka malo, nana e hume; nona ka malo, nau e hume, or 'Your malo he can wear; his malo you can wear.'"

David Malo - An early Maui historian and native Hawaiian scholar, teacher, and statesman who graduated from Lahain-aluna School in 1835 at the age of forty-two. Malo helped draft the Hawaiian declaration of rights and constitution, and he wrote an important record of traditional native practices, *Hawaiian Antiquities*. Thinking ahead to the Maui we now in-habit, he wrote: "If a big wave comes in, large and unfamiliar fishes will come from the dark ocean, and when they see the small fishes of the shallows they will eat them up."

Mana - Divine power, which is resident in rocks, bones, fin-gernail clippings, and all things of this divine world.

Maui Land & Pineapple Company - See A&B. The implosion of Maui Land & Pine has been one of the most important and least reported twists of Maui history in the early twenty-first century.

Mauka/makai - Basic directions for island-living people in Hawai'i. "Ma-uka" means literally "toward the mountain." "Ma-kai" means "toward the ocean." Mainland-style direc-tions: "Take Highway 360 east to the corner of Kalo Road and turn right." Maui-style directions: "Go Hana side to mile marker thirty-one, then go mauka."

language that listens to the forces above us. How many words do you have for the rain in your neighborhood?

Stink-eye - The vicious, murderous stare of death.

Ti (ki) - Another of those plants like taro that the Polynesians brought with them when they traveled, a kind of Dracaena bush that makes everyone happy with its big cool gladsome leaves that you can wear if you like. (No longer suitable as everyday attire.)

Tilapia - A type of fish that thrives in brackish water, mud puddles, ditches, bogs, murky ponds, and discarded saucepans.

Tutu - Grandma; grandma-like person.

Upcountry - The mountain country of East Maui, a loose geographical term with no precise boundaries; a mental state with no precise definition.

sometimes a crone, never one to be played with—is the face of fire, specifically the immortal embodiment of the volcanic ooze and spew of red-hot rock-fire. She's been kicking it up at Kilauea (Hawai'i Island) since 1983, having abandoned Haleakala some time ago. The exact place where she departed from Maui—having lost a battle-to-the-end with her sister the quenching sea—is a pu'u called Ka Iwi o Pele (Pele's bones) located just south of Hana Bay. By the way, Koki Beach, located right next to this pu'u, is excellent for body surfing.

Piko - Belly button. Omphalos. Center of the universe.

Poi - Perfectly nutritious substance made by mashing cooked kalo root. The bread-and-butter of old Hawai'i.

Poi dog - The kind of dog suitable for ancient Hawaiian barbecues, fattened all soft and tender because they've been eating poi. Lucky dogs.

Pono - good, morally right, excellent.

Pu'u - Cinder cone; small rounded hill formed by the blowing-out of billions of bits of fluffy lava. A typical feature of Maui's volcanic rift zones.

Rain - *Ua* (in Hawaiian). As an after-thought to the third essay in this collection, I feel it's important to point out that the rain that hits the top of your head is personal. When rain hits your next-door neighbor's house but not yours, that feels personal. The rain that drives sideways to slam against the left side of your house today is clearly a different rain from the one that slinks in sexily to coat the right side of your house tomorrow. The Hawaiian language has hundreds of words for rain. Several refer to rain that comes somehow to earth out of an utterly cloudless sky. Any language that pays attention to the sky is a

Made in the USA
Middletown, DE
26 April 2015